PYTHON FOR ENGINEERS

Applied Programming in Engineering Fields

THOMPSON CARTER

TABLE OF CONTENTS

<u>INTRODUCTION</u>..<u>7</u>

PYTHON FOR ENGINEERS: APPLIED PROGRAMMING IN ENGINEERING
FIELDS...7
WHY PYTHON FOR ENGINEERS? 8
A PRACTICAL, APPLIED APPROACH...8
REAL-WORLD ENGINEERING EXAMPLES 10
WHO THIS BOOK IS FOR..10
WHAT YOU WILL LEARN 11
WHY PYTHON IS THE FUTURE OF ENGINEERING 12

<u>CHAPTER 1: INTRODUCTION TO PYTHON FOR ENGINEERS</u>
....<u>14</u>

<u>CHAPTER 2: PYTHON BASICS – FOUNDATION FOR</u>
<u>ENGINEERING APPLICATIONS</u> ....<u>22</u>

<u>CHAPTER 3: HANDLING DATA – LISTS, TUPLES, AND</u>
<u>DICTIONARIES</u> ....<u>28</u>

<u>CHAPTER 4: MATHEMATICAL OPERATIONS AND LINEAR</u>
<u>ALGEBRA IN PYTHON</u> ....<u>35</u>

<u>CHAPTER 5: ENGINEERING SIMULATIONS – USING</u>
<u>PYTHON FOR NUMERICAL METHODS</u>...................................<u>42</u>

CHAPTER 6: PLOTTING AND DATA VISUALIZATION FOR ENGINEERS 50

CHAPTER 7: WORKING WITH ENGINEERING DATA – FILES AND DATABASES 54

KEY TAKEAWAYS 61

CHAPTER 8: OPTIMIZATION TECHNIQUES IN ENGINEERING 62

CHAPTER 9: AUTOMATION IN ENGINEERING – AUTOMATING REPETITIVE TASKS 71

CHAPTER 10: SIMULATION MODELING IN ENGINEERING WITH PYTHON 78

CHAPTER 11: SIGNAL PROCESSING IN ENGINEERING WITH PYTHON 85

CHAPTER 12: CONTROL SYSTEMS – MODELING AND SIMULATION 93

CHAPTER 13: STRUCTURAL ENGINEERING – ANALYZING AND MODELING STRUCTURES 101

CHAPTER 14: ELECTRICAL ENGINEERING – CIRCUIT SIMULATION 107

CHAPTER 15: MECHANICAL ENGINEERING – FLUID DYNAMICS AND THERMODYNAMICS.....................................116

CHAPTER 16: ROBOTICS PROGRAMMING IN PYTHON.......124

CHAPTER 17: PYTHON FOR CIVIL ENGINEERING – SURVEYING AND SITE ANALYSIS...132

CHAPTER 18: MACHINE LEARNING FOR ENGINEERING ...139

CHAPTER 19: DATA SCIENCE FOR ENGINEERING – DATA COLLECTION, CLEANING, AND ANALYSIS 147

INTRODUCTION TO DATA SCIENCE IN ENGINEERING 148
KEY LIBRARIES FOR DATA SCIENCE IN ENGINEERING.............................149
REAL-WORLD EXAMPLE: CLEANING AND ANALYZING SENSOR DATA 150

CHAPTER 20: PYTHON FOR ENVIRONMENTAL ENGINEERING...155

CHAPTER 21: COMPUTATIONAL FLUID DYNAMICS (CFD) WITH PYTHON 162

CHAPTER 22: IMAGE PROCESSING IN ENGINEERING APPLICATIONS 169

CHAPTER 23: PARALLEL PROGRAMMING IN ENGINEERING 176

CHAPTER 24: PYTHON IN ENGINEERING DESIGN AND CAD SYSTEMS 183

CHAPTER 25: FUTURE TRENDS – PYTHON IN EMERGING ENGINEERING FIELDS...189

CHAPTER 26: PYTHON FOR AUTOMATION AND SMART MANUFACTURING...199

CHAPTER 27: PYTHON FOR ENGINEERING DATA SECURITY AND PRIVACY 208

Introduction

Python for Engineers: Applied Programming in Engineering Fields

In recent years, Python has become an indispensable tool in the engineering world. Known for its simplicity, readability, and vast ecosystem of libraries, Python has rapidly evolved from a scripting language to a powerhouse for tackling a wide range of complex engineering challenges. Whether you're an electrical engineer analyzing circuit data, a mechanical engineer simulating fluid dynamics, or a civil engineer designing large-scale infrastructure projects, Python provides the versatility and power needed to streamline workflows, enhance productivity, and unlock new possibilities.

This book, ***Python for Engineers: Applied Programming in Engineering Fields***, is designed to introduce engineers from various disciplines to the world of Python programming, focusing specifically on how it can be applied to solve real-world engineering problems. The goal is to empower you with the skills to leverage Python for tackling engineering challenges—be it through automation, simulations, data analysis, or designing advanced systems. Each chapter is structured to provide you with a deep understanding of the fundamental concepts of Python, while highlighting the specific applications relevant to the engineering field you specialize in.

Why Python for Engineers?

Engineers are increasingly faced with the need to handle large datasets, automate repetitive tasks, and model complex systems. Traditionally, engineers have relied on specialized software or programming languages to accomplish these tasks. However, Python's accessibility, broad library support, and community-driven development make it an ideal language for engineers to incorporate into their toolkit. From automating design calculations to running advanced simulations and visualizing results, Python can help engineers increase efficiency, reduce errors, and gain deeper insights into their work.

In addition, Python integrates seamlessly with other engineering tools and platforms. For example, Python can communicate with databases, handle sensor data, interface with hardware (e.g., robotics, PLCs, IoT devices), and even work with machine learning frameworks to make predictions based on engineering data. With a growing ecosystem of Python libraries specifically designed for engineering applications—such as NumPy, SciPy, Matplotlib, Pandas, TensorFlow, and more—the potential for using Python to solve engineering problems is virtually limitless.

A Practical, Applied Approach

This book is not about just learning Python syntax. While we will cover the essential concepts of Python programming, our primary focus will be on how to apply Python to solve problems engineers encounter every day. Through hands-on examples and real-world applications, you will learn how to use Python for tasks such as:

- **Automation and Process Control:** Automating repetitive calculations and tasks in areas like structural analysis, circuit design, or system modeling.
- **Simulation and Modeling:** Using Python to create simulations for various engineering systems, from mechanical systems to fluid dynamics to electrical circuits.
- **Data Analysis and Visualization:** Collecting, cleaning, analyzing, and visualizing large datasets, such as sensor data, experimental results, or simulation outputs.
- **Optimization:** Implementing optimization techniques to improve efficiency in design, resource allocation, or manufacturing processes.
- **Machine Learning and AI:** Applying machine learning algorithms to predict behaviors, analyze patterns, or optimize engineering solutions.

The book is divided into topics that reflect the core areas of engineering, with each chapter focusing on a specific area of application. You'll learn how to approach engineering problems methodically, first by acquiring the programming skills needed to manipulate data and perform computations, and then by understanding how to use Python in conjunction with specialized engineering libraries to create solutions.

Real-World Engineering Examples

Each chapter includes practical, real-world examples relevant to engineering fields, demonstrating how Python can be applied to solve common engineering problems. For example, you'll learn how to use Python to:

- Automate the collection of sensor data and adjust machinery settings in a smart factory.
- Simulate fluid flow in mechanical systems or electrical circuit behavior.
- Analyze large datasets from experiments or real-time systems to derive meaningful insights.
- Build control systems that model and simulate engineering applications like robotics or PID controllers.

These examples are designed to provide engineers with the tools they need to create real-world applications and solve practical problems. By the end of this book, you'll be equipped not only with Python programming skills but also with the ability to apply those skills effectively in an engineering context.

Who This Book Is For

This book is intended for engineers from a variety of fields, including mechanical, civil, electrical, chemical, and robotics, who want to learn Python programming and apply it to their work. Whether you are a student looking to enhance your engineering education with Python or a professional engineer seeking to improve your computational skills, this book will guide you through the essential Python concepts and show you how they relate directly to the challenges you face in your field.

While no prior programming experience is necessary, familiarity with engineering concepts will be helpful. If you are new to Python, the book starts with the basics—introducing Python syntax and essential programming concepts—before progressing to more advanced topics like numerical methods, optimization, and machine learning. As you advance through the chapters, you will encounter examples, exercises, and case studies designed to reinforce key concepts and build your confidence in applying Python to engineering problems.

What You Will Learn

By the end of this book, you will have a solid understanding of:

1. **Python Programming Fundamentals:** Syntax, data types, functions, and control structures essential for any programming task.

2. **Engineering-Specific Libraries:** How to use libraries such as NumPy, SciPy, Matplotlib, and Pandas to tackle engineering problems related to data analysis, simulation, and optimization.

3. **Numerical Methods and Simulations:** Techniques for solving engineering equations numerically, modeling physical systems, and simulating real-world processes.

4. **Data Handling and Visualization:** How to work with large datasets, clean and preprocess data, and visualize results to gain insights into engineering problems.

5. **Automation and Control Systems:** Using Python to automate tasks, control machinery, and build embedded systems for engineering applications.

6. **Machine Learning and AI in Engineering:** Applying machine learning techniques to make predictions and optimize designs based on data.

Why Python is the Future of Engineering

Python's importance in engineering is only expected to grow. As industries move toward Industry 4.0—characterized by smarter automation, connectivity, and data-driven decision-making—the need for engineers to have programming skills has become more critical. Python's role in automating workflows, integrating with IIoT devices, and analyzing large datasets positions it as a key tool for engineers in the modern age.

This book aims to bridge the gap between traditional engineering practices and the cutting-edge technologies that are shaping the future. By learning Python and how it applies to engineering, you will be preparing yourself to take advantage of the incredible opportunities technology presents in the ever-evolving field of engineering.

Get ready to unlock the power of Python and transform the way you approach engineering challenges.

Chapter 1: Introduction to Python for Engineers

Why Python for Engineers?

In the modern world of engineering, programming plays a crucial role in solving complex problems, optimizing systems, and automating tasks. Among the various programming languages available, **Python** has risen to prominence, especially in the fields of engineering. Its simplicity, readability, and vast ecosystem of libraries make it an ideal choice for engineers who wish to leverage the power of programming without getting bogged down by the complexities of other languages.

Python's Simplicity and Versatility in Engineering Fields

Python is renowned for its **simple syntax**, which is both human-readable and concise. This simplicity allows engineers to focus more on problem-solving rather than on dealing with complex programming concepts. Python's versatile nature is particularly evident in its ability to handle a wide range of tasks across different engineering domains—from simulation and modeling to data analysis and control systems.

Engineers in fields such as **mechanical engineering**, **civil engineering**, **electrical engineering**, **chemical engineering**, and **aerospace engineering** have adopted Python to streamline their workflows. Whether it's performing mathematical calculations, simulating systems, or creating visualization tools, Python has proven to be an indispensable tool for engineering tasks.

- **Mechanical Engineering:** Python is used for simulations, numerical modeling, and control systems. Libraries like **NumPy** and **SciPy** are useful for performing scientific calculations and solving differential equations.
- **Civil Engineering:** In civil engineering, Python aids in structural analysis, optimization of construction processes, and geotechnical modeling. Tools like **Pandas** and **matplotlib** are widely used for data handling and visualization.
- **Electrical Engineering:** Python is used for digital signal processing, circuit analysis, and simulation. Libraries such as **SymPy** and **PySpice** are popular for electrical system modeling and simulation.
- **Chemical Engineering:** Python helps in process simulation, process control, and optimization. **Cantera** and **SciPy** are frequently used for solving problems related to chemical processes.
- **Aerospace Engineering:** Python assists in flight dynamics, trajectory optimization, and aerospace simulations. Libraries like **SciPy** and **matplotlib** help engineers analyze flight data and visualize results.

Overview of the Engineering Disciplines Where Python is Applied

Python's flexibility allows it to be applied across a vast array of engineering fields. Below is a of some key areas where Python has made significant inroads:

1. **Finite Element Analysis (FEA):** Engineers use Python for solving large-scale FEA problems that involve the simulation of physical phenomena like stress, heat transfer, and fluid flow. Libraries like **PyMesh** and **FEniCS** allow engineers to develop custom solvers or interface with industry-standard tools.

2. **Control Systems:** In control theory and automation, Python is used for developing control algorithms, simulating systems, and analyzing feedback loops. Libraries such as **control** and **scipy.signal** help in solving differential equations and analyzing stability.

3. **Data Science and Machine Learning:** Python is one of the most popular languages for data analysis, machine learning, and artificial intelligence. Engineers in various disciplines use Python to process data, apply statistical models, and develop predictive analytics. Libraries like **Pandas**, **NumPy**, **Scikit-learn**, and **TensorFlow** provide the necessary tools for these tasks.

4. **Optimization Problems:** In many engineering problems, optimization plays a key role—whether it's minimizing

energy consumption, optimizing design parameters, or maximizing system performance. Python's **SciPy** and **PuLP** libraries allow engineers to solve linear, nonlinear, and mixed-integer optimization problems.

5. **Simulation and Modeling:** Whether it's simulating fluid dynamics, electrical circuits, or mechanical systems, Python is a go-to language for creating accurate models of complex systems. Libraries like **SimPy** and **PySCeS** are popular choices for simulation.

6. **Visualization:** Python excels at turning complex data into visual insights, which is critical for engineers to interpret the results of simulations and data analysis. Libraries like **matplotlib**, **seaborn**, and **Plotly** provide powerful tools for creating everything from simple plots to interactive visualizations.

Setting Up Python for Engineering

Before diving into the coding aspect of Python, it's essential to set up the development environment that will allow you to write and execute Python code effectively. The process of setting up Python on your machine is straightforward, and this chapter will guide you through the steps to get started.

Installing Python and Relevant Libraries

1. **Installing Python:**

    o **Windows:** Download Python from the official website (https://www.python.org/), and run the installer. During installation, ensure that the "Add Python to PATH" option is checked to make Python globally accessible from the command line.

    o **macOS:** Python comes pre-installed on macOS, but you can install the latest version using **Homebrew** (brew install python) for easy management.

    o **Linux:** Python is often pre-installed on Linux distributions. However, if needed, you can install the latest version via the terminal (sudo apt install python3 on Ubuntu, for example).

2. **Installing Libraries:** Python's power comes from its ecosystem of libraries, which extend its functionality for specific tasks. Using Python's package manager, **pip**, you can easily install libraries for engineering-specific tasks.

    o Open a terminal or command prompt and use the following command to install popular engineering libraries:

    bash

    pip install numpy scipy matplotlib pandas sympy

3. These libraries are crucial for numerical computations, data analysis, and visualization.

4. **Setting Up a Virtual Environment:** To manage dependencies for specific projects, it's recommended to set up a **virtual environment**. This will help isolate libraries and avoid conflicts between different projects. To set up a virtual environment:

   o Navigate to your project directory in the terminal and run:

   bash

   python -m venv myenv

   o Activate the environment:
     - **Windows:** myenv\Scripts\activate
     - **macOS/Linux:** source myenv/bin/activate
   o Now, you can install the required libraries within this environment.

Setting Up an IDE and Development Environment

While you can write Python code in any text editor, using an Integrated Development Environment (IDE) will streamline the process with features like auto-completion, syntax highlighting, and integrated debugging tools.

- **VS Code:** A popular lightweight code editor with great support for Python. Install the **Python extension** for features like IntelliSense and debugging.
- **PyCharm:** A full-fledged IDE specifically designed for Python development, offering powerful tools for managing projects, running tests, and navigating large codebases.

Your First Python Program: "Hello, World!"

Let's write your first Python program! This simple program will print "Hello, World!" to the console. Open your IDE or text editor and create a new file called hello_world.py. Add the following code:

python

```python
print("Hello, World!")
```

To run the program:

- Open the terminal or command prompt.
- Navigate to the directory where your file is saved.
- Run the program by typing:

bash

```bash
python hello_world.py
```

You should see the output:

Hello, World!

Congratulations! You've just written and executed your first Python program.

In this chapter, we introduced Python's role in engineering, its versatility across various engineering disciplines, and how to set up the necessary tools to start coding. As we progress in this book, we will build on this foundation and dive deeper into applying Python to solve real-world engineering problems.

Chapter 2: Python Basics – Foundation for Engineering Applications

Python Syntax and Structure

Before diving into more complex engineering applications, it's essential to understand the **basic syntax** of Python. These foundational concepts are key to writing efficient, readable, and functional Python code for any engineering task.

Variables, Data Types, Loops, and Conditionals

- **Variables** are used to store data values. In Python, you don't need to declare a variable's type; Python automatically assigns it based on the value you store. For example:

python

```
mass = 10  # mass is an integer
velocity = 5.5  # velocity is a float
```

- **Data Types**: Python supports several built-in data types, including:
    - **Integers** (int), for whole numbers.
    - **Floats** (float), for decimal numbers.
    - **Strings** (str), for text-based data.
    - **Booleans** (bool), for true/false values.

- ○ **Lists** and **Tuples** for storing multiple values.
- **Loops**: Loops are used to execute a block of code multiple times.
  - ○ **For loop**: Useful for iterating over a sequence (like a list or a range of numbers). Example:

    python

    ```python
    for i in range(5):  # Loops 5 times
        print(i)
    ```

  - ○ **While loop**: Runs as long as a condition is true. Example:

    python

    ```python
    i = 0
    while i < 5:
        print(i)
        i += 1  # Increment i to avoid infinite loop
    ```

- **Conditionals**: Conditional statements (if, else, elif) allow you to perform different actions based on specific conditions. Example:

  python

  ```python
  temperature = 30
  if temperature > 25:
  ```

```
    print("It's hot outside!")
else:
    print("It's a nice day.")
```

Functions, Modules, and Basic I/O

- **Functions**: Functions are essential for organizing code and reusing logic. A function is a block of code that performs a specific task. Example:

  python

  ```python
  def calculate_force(mass, acceleration):
      return mass * acceleration
  ```

  You can call this function with different inputs:

  python

  ```python
  force = calculate_force(10, 9.8)
  print(f"The force is: {force} N")
  ```

- **Modules**: Python allows you to organize your code into modules, which are reusable pieces of code. You can import built-in or external modules into your program. For example, using the math module for mathematical operations:

  python

  ```python
  import math
  ```

```
result = math.sqrt(16)  # Calculates the square root
print(result)
```

- **Basic Input/Output (I/O)**: Handling input and output is crucial for interacting with users or other systems. Python provides simple functions for input and output.
  - **Input**: You can take user input using the input() function, which returns the input as a string. For example:

    python

    ```
    radius = float(input("Enter the radius: "))  # Takes input and converts it to a float
    ```

  - **Output**: You can display information using print():

    python

    ```
    print("The area is:", area)
    ```

Practical Engineering Example

Now that we've covered the Python basics, let's put these concepts into practice by writing a simple Python program that calculates force or velocity, both of which are fundamental concepts in engineering.

Let's assume you want to calculate **force (F)** using Newton's second law of motion:

F=m×aF = m \times aF=m×a

Where:

- **F** is the force (in Newtons).
- **m** is the mass (in kilograms).
- **a** is the acceleration (in meters per second squared).

We'll create a Python program that takes **mass** and **acceleration** as inputs, and then computes the force.

Here's the code:

python

```
# Function to calculate force
def calculate_force(mass, acceleration):
    return mass * acceleration

# Taking inputs from the user
mass = float(input("Enter the mass (kg): "))
acceleration = float(input("Enter the acceleration (m/s^2): "))

# Calculate the force
force = calculate_force(mass, acceleration)

# Output the result
```

```
print(f"The force is: {force} N")
```

Explanation of the Code:

- We define a function calculate_force() that takes two parameters (mass and acceleration) and returns the calculated force.
- We then use the input() function to take user inputs for mass and acceleration, converting these to float type (to handle decimal values).
- Finally, we print the result using print() to display the calculated force.

Real-World Scenario: In engineering, this basic formula for calculating force can be applied to a wide range of scenarios, from mechanical design to structural analysis. For example, civil engineers may need to calculate the forces acting on a bridge, or mechanical engineers may need to compute the force generated by a moving object in a system.

This is just the beginning, and as you advance through this book, you'll see how these foundational concepts can be applied to more complex engineering problems.

Chapter 3: Handling Data – Lists, Tuples, and Dictionaries

In engineering, data handling is a crucial aspect of problem-solving, whether you're dealing with sensor readings, measurements, or project-related data. Python provides several powerful data structures, each suited for different kinds of data storage and manipulation tasks. This chapter will explore **lists**, **tuples**, and **dictionaries**, which are essential for handling data in engineering applications.

Understanding and Using Data Structures

1. Lists

A **list** is an ordered collection of items that can be changed (mutable). It allows you to store multiple items in a single variable. Lists can hold data of different types, including numbers, strings, and other lists.

- **Creating Lists**: Lists are created by enclosing items in square brackets []. Items in a list are separated by commas.

    python

    temperatures = [22.5, 23.0, 23.5, 24.0, 24.5] # A list of temperatures

- **Accessing and Manipulating Lists**: You can access list items by index (starting from 0) and manipulate lists with functions like .append(), .remove(), and .sort().

python

```
print(temperatures[0])  # Output: 22.5
temperatures.append(25.0)  # Add a new temperature
temperatures.sort()  # Sort the list in ascending order
```

- **Practical Use in Engineering**: In engineering, lists are ideal when you need an ordered collection of values that can change, such as the series of readings from a temperature sensor.

Example:

python

```
sensor_readings = [12.4, 15.7, 19.3, 20.5, 21.1]
avg_temperature = sum(sensor_readings) / len(sensor_readings)  # Calculate average temperature
print(f"Average Temperature: {avg_temperature}")
```

2. Tuples

A **tuple** is similar to a list but is **immutable**, meaning that once a tuple is created, its contents cannot be changed. Tuples are often used to store data that shouldn't be modified, making them ideal for representing fixed data sets.

- **Creating Tuples**: Tuples are defined using parentheses ():

python

point = (3, 4) # A 2D coordinate point

- **Accessing Items**: You can access tuple items just like lists using indexing:

python

print(point[0]) # Output: 3

- **Practical Use in Engineering**: Tuples are used for fixed sets of data, like coordinates, points in 3D space, or a set of constants. For example, a point in a 3D coordinate system is often represented by a tuple (x, y, z).

Example:

python

sensor_position = (10, 20, 5) # x, y, z position of a sensor in 3D space

3. Dictionaries

A **dictionary** is an unordered collection of data stored as key-value pairs. Dictionaries are highly useful when you want to associate specific values with a label (key). They are perfect for situations where you need to retrieve data based on some identifier, such as looking up specific sensor data using a device ID or time stamp.

- **Creating Dictionaries**: Dictionaries are created using curly braces {} with key-value pairs separated by a colon:

python

```python
sensor_data = {'temperature': 22.5, 'pressure': 1012, 'humidity': 55}
```

- **Accessing Data**: You can access the values in a dictionary using their keys:

python

```python
print(sensor_data['temperature'])  # Output: 22.5
```

- **Practical Use in Engineering**: Dictionaries are ideal for scenarios where you need to associate a value (e.g., sensor reading) with a specific key (e.g., sensor name, time, or location). For instance, when monitoring different sensors in a plant, you could store data for each sensor as a dictionary with unique identifiers.

Example:

python

```python
sensor_data = {'sensor_1': {'temperature': 22.5, 'humidity': 55},
```

'sensor_2': {'temperature': 23.0, 'humidity': 60}}

```
# Access temperature from sensor 1
print(sensor_data['sensor_1']['temperature'])  # Output: 22.5
```

Choosing the Right Data Structure for Engineering Tasks

- **Lists** are best used for ordered data that can change, such as time series data, sensor readings, or measurements taken over a period.
- **Tuples** are perfect for immutable data, like fixed parameters or sensor locations.
- **Dictionaries** excel when you need to map a key (e.g., a sensor ID) to a value (e.g., sensor readings or conditions).

Real-World Example: Storing and Analyzing Sensor Data from an Engineering Device

In engineering, you often deal with real-time data from sensors, such as temperature, pressure, and humidity readings. These sensors collect a variety of measurements, and you need to store and process them efficiently.

Task: Write a Python program to store and analyze sensor data collected from multiple devices in a factory. The program should calculate the average temperature and identify sensors that are reporting temperatures outside of the desired range.

Step 1: Store the sensor data in a dictionary. Each sensor will have a unique ID, and its readings will be stored as a list of temperature values.

python

```
sensor_data = {
    'sensor_1': [22.5, 23.0, 24.1, 21.5, 22.8],
    'sensor_2': [25.5, 26.0, 25.8, 26.3, 27.0],
    'sensor_3': [20.1, 19.5, 20.2, 21.0, 21.5],
}
```

Step 2: Calculate the average temperature for each sensor.

python

```
def average_temperature(temperatures):
    return sum(temperatures) / len(temperatures)

for sensor_id, temperatures in sensor_data.items():
    avg_temp = average_temperature(temperatures)
    print(f"Average Temperature for {sensor_id}: {avg_temp}°C")
```

Step 3: Identify sensors with temperatures outside the desired range (e.g., 20°C to 25°C).

python

```
out_of_range_sensors = []

for sensor_id, temperatures in sensor_data.items():
    avg_temp = average_temperature(temperatures)
```

```
    if avg_temp < 20 or avg_temp > 25:
        out_of_range_sensors.append(sensor_id)

if out_of_range_sensors:
    print(f"Sensors out of range: {', '.join(out_of_range_sensors)}")
else:
    print("All sensors are within the acceptable temperature range.")
```

Output Example:

yaml

Average Temperature for sensor_1: 22.98°C

Average Temperature for sensor_2: 26.12°C

Average Temperature for sensor_3: 20.66°C

Sensors out of range: sensor_2

Understanding how to store and manipulate data effectively is foundational for solving engineering problems. By using the appropriate data structures, such as lists, tuples, and dictionaries, you can handle various types of engineering data and perform necessary calculations or analyses. As you advance in Python, these structures will serve as the building blocks for more complex engineering applications.

Chapter 4: Mathematical Operations and Linear Algebra in Python

In engineering, mathematical computations are at the core of many tasks, from structural analysis to data modeling. Python, with its powerful libraries such as **NumPy** and **SciPy**, provides an easy-to-use environment for engineers to perform complex mathematical operations and linear algebra tasks efficiently.

This chapter will guide you through the mathematical tools available in Python and demonstrate how to apply them to real-world engineering problems. By the end of this chapter, you will be equipped to solve engineering-related mathematical problems, perform matrix operations, and use advanced mathematical functions in your projects.

Mathematical Libraries: NumPy and SciPy

1. Introduction to NumPy for Engineering Math

NumPy (Numerical Python) is the foundational library for numerical computing in Python. It offers fast, vectorized operations on large data arrays and matrices, making it a vital tool for engineers working with numerical data.

- **What is NumPy?** NumPy provides an array object called ndarray that can store large datasets efficiently. It also includes functions for mathematical operations like addition, multiplication, and statistical operations on arrays.

- **Creating Arrays with NumPy** The primary object in NumPy is the ndarray, a multidimensional array object that stores homogeneous data. You can create arrays from lists or tuples using the numpy.array() function.

python

```
import numpy as np
# Creating a one-dimensional array
temperatures = np.array([22.5, 23.0, 23.5, 24.0])

# Creating a two-dimensional array (matrix)
matrix = np.array([[1, 2, 3], [4, 5, 6], [7, 8, 9]])
```

- **Basic Array Operations** NumPy arrays support vectorized operations, meaning you can perform mathematical operations element-wise on the array. This eliminates the need for loops, making the code more readable and efficient.

python

```
# Element-wise addition
temperatures = temperatures + 1.5
```

```
# Matrix addition
result = matrix + matrix
```

- **Linear Algebra Operations** NumPy provides several functions for performing linear algebra operations such as dot products, matrix multiplication, and matrix inversion.

python

```
# Matrix multiplication
dot_product = np.dot(matrix, matrix.T)

# Matrix inversion (for solving linear systems)
matrix_inv = np.linalg.inv(matrix)
```

2. Using SciPy for More Complex Mathematical Computations

SciPy builds on NumPy and provides a wide range of functions for more advanced mathematical operations such as optimization, integration, interpolation, and solving differential equations. SciPy is especially useful in engineering when dealing with complex algorithms or performing scientific computations.

- **What is SciPy?** SciPy is a library that offers functions for scientific and technical computing. It integrates seamlessly with NumPy, and many of SciPy's modules are designed for optimization, signal processing, statistics, and linear algebra.

- **Key SciPy Modules for Engineering**
  - **scipy.linalg**: A module for advanced linear algebra (e.g., solving systems of linear equations).
  - **scipy.optimize**: Provides functions for optimization tasks such as minimizing or maximizing objective functions.
  - **scipy.integrate**: Includes functions for numerical integration (e.g., solving ordinary differential equations).
- **Example: Solving Linear Systems** In mechanical engineering, you might need to solve a system of linear equations to determine forces in a structure. SciPy's linalg.solve() function allows you to solve linear systems of equations.

python

```
from scipy.linalg import solve
# Coefficient matrix A
A = np.array([[3, 2], [1, 2]])

# Right-hand side vector b
b = np.array([10, 12])

# Solving for x (Ax = b)
x = solve(A, b)
print(x)
```

This example solves for x in the equation Ax=bAx = bAx=b, where AAA is the coefficient matrix and bbb is the right-hand side vector.

- **Example: Optimization Problems** In engineering, you may need to optimize certain parameters, such as minimizing material cost or maximizing structural integrity. SciPy's optimize.minimize() function helps find the optimal values of variables.

python

```
from scipy.optimize import minimize

# Define the objective function (e.g., cost function)
def objective(x):
    return x[0]**2 + x[1]**2 + 10  # simple quadratic function

# Initial guess for x
initial_guess = [1, 1]

# Minimize the objective function
result = minimize(objective, initial_guess)
print(result.x)  # Optimal values of x
```

Real-World Example: Matrix Operations for Mechanical Engineering Simulations

In mechanical engineering, simulations often require solving systems of linear equations and performing matrix operations. For example, you might need to compute the displacement of a structure under load using the finite element method (FEM).

- **Example: Solving for Displacement in a Mechanical Structure**

  Consider a simple 2D static structure where we want to calculate the displacement of the nodes using a stiffness matrix. The basic formula for FEM is:

  $[K] \cdot [u] = [F][K] \cdot [u] = [F][K] \cdot [u] = [F]$

  Where:

  - $[K][K][K]$ is the global stiffness matrix.
  - $[u][u][u]$ is the displacement vector.
  - $[F][F][F]$ is the force vector.

  We can solve this equation using the following Python code:

  python

```
# Define the stiffness matrix (K)
K = np.array([[4, -2], [-2, 4]])

# Define the force vector (F)
```

```
F = np.array([0, 10])

# Solve for displacement (u)
displacement = solve(K, F)
print("Displacement:", displacement)
```

This code calculates the displacement of the two nodes in the structure under the applied force, assuming a simple 2D scenario.

This chapter covered the basics of mathematical operations and linear algebra in Python, focusing on the core libraries that engineers can use for their calculations: **NumPy** and **SciPy**. You learned how to create and manipulate arrays, perform matrix operations, and solve real-world engineering problems like solving linear systems and optimizing parameters. These tools will be invaluable for engineering simulations, whether you're working in mechanical, electrical, or civil engineering.

In the next chapter, we will explore how to work with **data visualization** to graphically represent the results of your mathematical computations and simulations.

Chapter 5: Engineering Simulations – Using Python for Numerical Methods

In engineering, numerical methods are indispensable tools for solving complex problems that cannot be solved analytically. From structural mechanics to fluid dynamics, engineers often rely on numerical simulations to model real-world systems, make predictions, and optimize designs. Python, with its extensive libraries and user-friendly syntax, is a perfect language for implementing and testing numerical methods in engineering.

In this chapter, we will dive into various numerical methods used in engineering simulations. We will introduce the core techniques and apply them to solve real-world engineering problems. By the end of this chapter, you will have a solid understanding of how to use Python for numerical simulations, with practical examples to guide you in applying these methods to your own engineering challenges.

---

1. Introduction to Numerical Methods in Engineering

What Are Numerical Methods?

Numerical methods are mathematical techniques used to approximate solutions to mathematical problems that are too difficult or impossible to solve analytically. These methods are especially useful in engineering, where complex systems and models often require approximations. Some of the key applications of numerical methods include:

- **Solving equations**: For example, finding roots of equations or solving systems of linear equations.
- **Numerical integration**: Estimating the area under curves for functions that are difficult to integrate analytically.
- **Differentiation**: Calculating derivatives of functions at specific points.

Python's scientific libraries such as **NumPy** and **SciPy** provide efficient implementations of many of these numerical methods. We will focus on the following core techniques:

Root-Finding Methods

Root-finding methods are used to find solutions to equations where we want to determine the value of xxx such that $f(x)=0 f(x) = 0 f(x)=0$. The most common root-finding methods used in engineering include:

- **Bisection Method**: A simple but reliable method for solving continuous equations.
- **Newton's Method**: An iterative method for solving equations more efficiently, assuming the initial guess is close to the actual root.

Example: Solving a Simple Equation Using Newton's Method

python

```python
import numpy as np

# Define the function and its derivative
def f(x):
    return x**2 - 4

def df(x):
    return 2*x

# Implementing Newton's method
def newton_method(f, df, x0, tol=1e-6, max_iter=100):
    x = x0
    for i in range(max_iter):
        x_new = x - f(x) / df(x)
        if abs(x_new - x) < tol:
            return x_new
        x = x_new
    return x

# Initial guess
x0 = 2
root = newton_method(f, df, x0)
print(f"Root found: {root}")
```

In this example, we are using **Newton's Method** to solve the equation $x2−4=0x^2 - 4 = 0x2−4=0$, which has roots at $x=2x =$

2x=2 and x=−2x = -2x=−2. The method iteratively improves the guess until it converges to a solution.

Numerical Integration and Differentiation

Numerical integration is the process of approximating the value of an integral (area under a curve) when the function is difficult or impossible to integrate analytically. Common methods include:

- **Trapezoidal Rule**: Approximates the integral by breaking the area under the curve into trapezoids.
- **Simpson's Rule**: A more accurate method that approximates the integral using quadratic polynomials.

Numerical differentiation, on the other hand, involves approximating the derivative of a function. Common methods include:

- **Forward Difference**: Approximates the derivative by taking the difference between function values at nearby points.
- **Central Difference**: A more accurate method that takes the average of forward and backward differences.

Example: Numerical Integration Using the Trapezoidal Rule
python

```
# Define the function to integrate
def f(x):
```

```
    return np.sin(x)

# Trapezoidal rule for numerical integration
def trapezoidal_rule(f, a, b, n=1000):
    x = np.linspace(a, b, n)
    y = f(x)
    return (b - a) * (np.sum(y) - (y[0] + y[-1]) / 2) / (n - 1)

# Integrate sin(x) from 0 to pi
result = trapezoidal_rule(f, 0, np.pi)
print(f"Numerical integral of sin(x) from 0 to pi: {result}")
```

In this example, the **Trapezoidal Rule** is used to approximate the integral of $\sin(x)$\sin(x)sin(x) over the interval $[0, \pi]$. This method is simple yet effective, and it forms the foundation for more advanced numerical integration techniques.

---

2. Real-World Example – Solving Heat Transfer Problems in Python

In engineering, heat transfer problems are commonly encountered in fields such as mechanical engineering, aerospace engineering, and civil engineering. These problems often involve solving partial differential equations (PDEs) that describe the temperature distribution over time and space. Here, we will apply numerical methods to solve a simplified heat transfer problem using Python.

Heat Transfer Problem

Consider a one-dimensional heat conduction problem in a metal rod. The temperature at each point along the rod changes over time, and we want to find the temperature distribution after a certain time period. The governing equation for heat conduction is given by:

∂T∂t=α∂2T∂x2\frac{\partial T}{\partial t} = \alpha \frac{\partial^2 T}{\partial x^2}∂t∂T=α∂x2∂2T

Where:

- $T(x,t)T(x,t)T(x,t)$ is the temperature at point xxx and time ttt,
- α\alphaα is the thermal diffusivity constant.

We will use the **Finite Difference Method (FDM)** to discretize this equation and solve it numerically.

Example: Solving a Heat Transfer Problem Using FDM

python

```
import numpy as np
import matplotlib.pyplot as plt

# Parameters
L = 10.0  # Length of the rod
T0 = 100  # Initial temperature
alpha = 0.01  # Thermal diffusivity
Nx = 50  # Number of spatial divisions
```

```
Nt = 200  # Number of time steps
dx = L / (Nx - 1)  # Spatial step size
dt = 0.01  # Time step size

# Initialize temperature array
T = np.ones(Nx) * T0

# Boundary conditions
T[0] = T[Nx-1] = 0  # Fixed temperature at the ends

# Finite Difference Method
for t in range(1, Nt):
    T_new = T.copy()
    for i in range(1, Nx - 1):
        T_new[i] = T[i] + alpha * dt / dx**2 * (T[i-1] - 2*T[i] + T[i+1])
    T = T_new

# Plot the temperature distribution
x = np.linspace(0, L, Nx)
plt.plot(x, T)
plt.xlabel('Position along the rod (m)')
plt.ylabel('Temperature (°C)')
plt.title('Heat Distribution in the Rod')
plt.show()
```

In this example, we discretize the heat conduction equation using the **Finite Difference Method**. The boundary conditions specify that the ends of the rod are kept at a constant temperature of 0°C, and we solve for the temperature distribution at each time step.

3.

In this chapter, we have explored the fundamentals of numerical methods in engineering. We learned how to apply Python to solve problems such as root finding, numerical integration, and heat transfer simulations. With libraries like **NumPy** and **SciPy**, Python provides powerful tools for engineers to perform complex calculations and simulations efficiently.

By mastering these techniques, you can tackle a wide range of engineering problems, from structural analysis to thermal simulations, with confidence. In the next chapters, we will explore additional applications of Python in engineering, focusing on optimization, simulations, and more advanced numerical methods.

This chapter has provided the building blocks for solving engineering problems using Python. Whether you're working on fluid dynamics, structural mechanics, or heat transfer, Python's simplicity and power make it an invaluable tool for engineers.

Chapter 6: Plotting and Data Visualization for Engineers

In engineering, data visualization is not just about making pretty graphs—it's about communicating complex ideas, trends, and results effectively. Whether you're analyzing sensor data, simulating stress distributions, or plotting temperature gradients, visualization plays a key role in understanding and presenting engineering data. Python's powerful libraries like Matplotlib and Seaborn make it easy to visualize data in meaningful ways that can inform decisions and drive design.

This chapter will guide you through the fundamentals of plotting and data visualization, with a focus on tools and techniques that are particularly useful for engineers. We will explore how to create clear, informative graphs, from basic 2D plots to more advanced 3D visualizations, all while keeping engineering-specific challenges and requirements in mind.

Visualizing Data with Matplotlib and Seaborn

Python's Matplotlib library is the cornerstone of scientific plotting, allowing for fine-grained control over almost every aspect of your graphs. Seaborn, built on top of Matplotlib, offers a high-level interface for drawing attractive, informative statistical graphics.

1. **Introduction to Plotting in 2D and 3D:**

- o **2D Plots**: Learn how to plot basic graphs like line plots, scatter plots, bar charts, and histograms to analyze data trends or distributions.
- o **3D Plots**: Explore Matplotlib's capabilities for 3D plotting, essential for visualizing more complex data sets in engineering, such as surface plots or mesh plots used in stress analysis or fluid flow simulations.

2. **Customizing Graphs for Engineering Presentations:**

- o **Labels and Titles**: Learn how to customize axis labels, titles, and legends to ensure that your graphs are clear and professional.
- o **Gridlines and Axes**: Understand how to adjust gridlines, axis ticks, and limits for more precise control over the graph's appearance, especially in engineering contexts where precision is crucial.
- o **Color and Style**: Use color palettes effectively to highlight key data points or trends, and learn how to customize line styles, markers, and text annotations.

Real-World Example: Plotting Temperature Variations Across a Surface

To put these techniques into practice, we'll work through an example in which we plot temperature distribution across a material surface, a common problem in thermal engineering.

- **Problem Setup**: Suppose we are tasked with visualizing how temperature varies across a flat surface, such as a metal plate being heated. Temperature data could be collected from a series of sensors placed at different points on the surface.

- **Python Implementation**: We will use a 2D grid of temperature values and plot it using a contour plot, which is ideal for visualizing how a scalar field (temperature) changes across a surface. You'll learn how to:
  - Create the grid using NumPy.
  - Use Matplotlib's contour function to generate contour lines that represent temperature gradients.
  - Customize the plot for clarity and impact, making sure the color scale represents temperature variations accurately.

Real-World Example: Visualizing Stress Distribution in Materials

Another important application in engineering is the visualization of stress or strain distribution in materials, such as in structural or mechanical engineering.

- **Problem Setup**: Imagine a structural beam under various loading conditions, and we want to visualize the stress distribution across the beam's surface.

- **Python Implementation**: We will use a 3D surface plot to represent stress distribution over the beam. You will learn:
  - How to generate synthetic data representing stress values at different points on a 3D grid.
  - How to visualize this stress distribution using Matplotlib's plot_surface function.
  - Techniques for customizing the surface plot with proper labels, color maps, and view angles to improve interpretability.

Through these examples, you'll not only learn how to visualize engineering data effectively but also how to make your visualizations suitable for engineering analysis and presentations. Proper data visualization is an essential skill that will help you communicate your findings with clarity and precision, making it an invaluable tool in your engineering toolkit.

Chapter 7: Working with Engineering Data – Files and Databases

Engineers often work with large datasets that need to be processed, analyzed, and stored in a way that is efficient and organized. This chapter will focus on practical techniques for working with engineering data, including reading and writing files, and interacting with databases. We will look at how Python simplifies these tasks, allowing you to seamlessly store, retrieve, and manage engineering data, whether it's collected from experiments, simulations, or industrial systems.

Reading and Writing Files

In engineering, data often comes in various formats, including CSV files, Excel spreadsheets, and plain text logs. Python makes it easy to work with these file formats, offering a range of tools and libraries to handle data in a structured way.

- **Working with CSV Files:** CSV (Comma-Separated Values) is one of the most common formats for storing tabular data, especially when dealing with experimental or simulation data. Python's csv module provides a straightforward approach for reading and writing data to CSV files. The data can be loaded into a list or dictionary and then manipulated as needed.

Example: You could be collecting temperature readings from various sensors in a factory or laboratory. By storing this data in a CSV file, you can later process it for analysis or visualization.

- **Handling Excel Files:** Often, engineers work with Excel files for data storage and analysis. Python libraries like pandas can read and write Excel files, allowing for seamless data import and export between Python and Excel.

Example: An engineer conducting an analysis of material strength could store data like stress-strain curves or experimental results in an Excel sheet. Python's pandas can quickly import this data, perform necessary calculations, and save the results for further analysis.

- **Reading and Writing Plain Text Files:** Sometimes, engineers need to parse simple text files that contain logs, measurements, or reports. Python's built-in file handling methods allow you to read and write text files line by line, making it easy to extract specific information from unstructured data.

Example: A script that processes logs from a weather station could read from a plain text file, extract key data points such as temperature, humidity, and pressure, and save it in a more structured format for further analysis.

Example Code: Reading and Writing CSV Files

python

```python
import csv

# Reading data from a CSV file
with open('sensor_data.csv', mode='r') as file:
    csv_reader = csv.reader(file)
    for row in csv_reader:
        print(row)

# Writing data to a CSV file
data = [['Sensor', 'Temperature', 'Humidity'],
        ['Sensor 1', 22.4, 65],
        ['Sensor 2', 21.8, 60]]

with open('output_data.csv', mode='w', newline='') as file:
    csv_writer = csv.writer(file)
    csv_writer.writerows(data)
```

Database Interaction

When dealing with large datasets or data that needs to be queried and managed over time, using a database is essential. Python offers a range of database interaction libraries, with SQLite being a lightweight, file-based option that doesn't require a dedicated server.

SQLite is an excellent choice for smaller engineering applications, where you might be storing experimental data, sensor readings, or test results. It allows for structured storage of data in tables, and Python's sqlite3 module provides an easy interface to interact with SQLite databases.

Example Code: Using SQLite to Store Engineering Data

python

```python
import sqlite3

# Connecting to SQLite database (it will create the file if it doesn't exist)
conn = sqlite3.connect('engineering_data.db')
cursor = conn.cursor()

# Creating a table for storing sensor data
cursor.execute('''
CREATE TABLE IF NOT EXISTS sensor_readings (
    id INTEGER PRIMARY KEY,
    sensor_name TEXT,
    temperature REAL,
    humidity REAL
)
''')

# Inserting data into the table
cursor.execute('''
INSERT INTO sensor_readings (sensor_name, temperature, humidity)
VALUES ('Sensor 1', 22.4, 65)
''')

# Committing changes and closing the connection
```

```
conn.commit()

# Querying the data
cursor.execute('SELECT * FROM sensor_readings')
rows = cursor.fetchall()
for row in rows:
    print(row)

# Closing the connection
conn.close()
```

This code snippet demonstrates how to create an SQLite database, store sensor data in a table, and query the data using Python.

Real-World Example: Writing a Program to Log Experimental Data

In this section, we'll implement a real-world example where you write a Python program to log data from an engineering experiment, such as monitoring temperature and humidity levels over time. This program will collect data, store it in a CSV file or SQLite database, and provide basic data manipulation tools for analysis.

1. **Data Collection**: You could simulate data collection from a sensor or retrieve real-time data from an IoT device using Python. This can be done using libraries like random for generating data or libraries like pySerial for serial communication with sensors.

2. **Logging the Data**: The data will then be logged into a structured format (CSV or SQLite database), depending on your choice. You'll also implement a mechanism to regularly save the data, ensuring that the data is consistently updated and not lost.

3. **Analysis and Visualization**: Once the data is logged, the program can be extended to include basic analysis such as calculating averages, finding trends, or visualizing the data using libraries like Matplotlib.

Example of Logging and Analyzing Sensor Data:

python

```python
import random
import sqlite3
import time

# Simulate collecting sensor data
def collect_data():
    temperature = random.uniform(20.0, 30.0)  # Simulate temperature between 20 and 30
    humidity = random.uniform(40.0, 70.0)     # Simulate humidity between 40 and 70%
    return temperature, humidity

# Store the data in SQLite
def store_data(temperature, humidity):
    conn = sqlite3.connect('sensor_log.db')
    cursor = conn.cursor()
```

```
cursor.execute('''
CREATE TABLE IF NOT EXISTS sensor_logs (
    id INTEGER PRIMARY KEY,
    temperature REAL,
    humidity REAL,
    timestamp DATETIME DEFAULT CURRENT_TIMESTAMP
)
''')

cursor.execute('''
INSERT INTO sensor_logs (temperature, humidity)
VALUES (?, ?)
''', (temperature, humidity))

conn.commit()
conn.close()

# Log data every 5 seconds for 1 minute
for _ in range(12):
    temp, hum = collect_data()
    store_data(temp, hum)
    print(f"Logged data: Temperature={temp:.2f}, Humidity={hum:.2f}")
    time.sleep(5)

print("Data logging complete.")
```

In this example, the program simulates the collection of temperature and humidity data and logs it to an SQLite database every 5 seconds. This type of application could be useful for long-term monitoring in engineering projects, where sensor data needs to be logged over time for analysis.

Key Takeaways

- **File Handling**: Python simplifies the process of reading from and writing to various file formats like CSV and Excel, which is especially useful for engineers working with experimental data or simulations.
- **Database Management**: For more structured data handling, Python's sqlite3 module provides a lightweight and efficient way to store and query engineering data.
- **Real-World Applications**: From logging sensor data to storing it in a database, Python can be used to streamline data collection, storage, and analysis in real-world engineering scenarios.

By mastering these file and database handling techniques, engineers can efficiently manage their data, ensuring it's easy to access, analyze, and interpret in the future.

Chapter 8: Optimization Techniques in Engineering

Optimization is a cornerstone of engineering, used to improve efficiency, reduce costs, and enhance system performance across numerous disciplines. Whether you're optimizing material usage in structural design, minimizing energy consumption in manufacturing processes, or maximizing performance in computational models, optimization techniques are integral to solving real-world engineering problems. This chapter will introduce you to various optimization techniques and show how Python can be used to solve optimization problems using specialized libraries.

Introduction to Optimization Problems

Optimization problems are encountered in nearly every engineering field, whether you're designing a bridge, optimizing the performance of a mechanical system, or improving the efficiency of a chemical process. An optimization problem typically consists of the following components:

- **Objective Function:** A mathematical function that needs to be maximized or minimized. For example, minimizing material costs or maximizing the structural strength of a design.

- **Constraints:** Limitations or conditions that the solution must satisfy, such as structural integrity or energy consumption limits.
- **Decision Variables:** The variables that can be adjusted to optimize the objective function, such as the thickness of a material or the speed of a machine.

Optimization problems can be classified into several types:

1. **Linear Optimization (Linear Programming):** The objective function and constraints are linear. These problems are often solvable using algorithms like the Simplex method.
2. **Nonlinear Optimization:** The objective function or the constraints are nonlinear, making the problem more complex and requiring more advanced algorithms.
3. **Constrained Optimization:** There are specific restrictions or limitations that must be adhered to, such as maximum allowable stress in a material or design constraints.
4. **Unconstrained Optimization:** These problems do not have explicit constraints on the solution, allowing for greater flexibility in the optimization process.

Solvers in Python: SciPy, CVXPY, and Optimization Libraries

Python offers a variety of libraries and tools to tackle optimization problems, making it a go-to language for engineers who need to solve complex design and operational challenges. Below are some of the most widely used libraries for optimization tasks:

1. **SciPy Optimization:** The SciPy library is one of the most powerful tools in Python for scientific computing. It includes the optimize module, which provides functions for solving both linear and nonlinear optimization problems. The scipy.optimize module supports a range of algorithms like gradient descent, simplex methods, and interior-point methods. Here's an example of how you can use SciPy to solve a simple optimization problem:

python

```
import numpy as np
from scipy.optimize import minimize

# Define the objective function (minimize material cost)
def objective(x):
    return x[0]**2 + x[1]**2  # Simplified objective: minimize sum of squares of x

# Constraints: x[0] + x[1] = 5 (e.g., fixed material volume)
def constraint(x):
    return x[0] + x[1] - 5

# Initial guess
x0 = [1, 1]
```

```python
# Set up the constraints and bounds
cons = {'type': 'eq', 'fun': constraint}
result = minimize(objective, x0, constraints=cons)

print(result)
```

This example uses SciPy to minimize the sum of the squares of two variables $x[0]$ and $x[1]$, with a constraint that their sum equals 5.

2. **CVXPY for Convex Optimization:** For more advanced optimization problems, such as those encountered in control systems, signal processing, or machine learning, CVXPY is an excellent tool. It is designed specifically for convex optimization, making it easy to express and solve problems like linear programming (LP), quadratic programming (QP), and semidefinite programming (SDP).

Example code for solving a convex optimization problem with CVXPY:

python

```python
import cvxpy as cp

# Variables
x = cp.Variable()
y = cp.Variable()

# Objective function: minimize x^2 + y^2
```

```
objective = cp.Minimize(x**2 + y**2)

# Constraints: x + y == 5
constraints = [x + y == 5]

# Problem setup
problem = cp.Problem(objective, constraints)

# Solve the problem
problem.solve()

print("Optimal x:", x.value)
print("Optimal y:", y.value)
```

In this example, CVXPY optimizes two variables, x and y, subject to the constraint $x + y = 5$.

3. **Other Optimization Libraries:**

   o **Pyomo:** A Python-based open-source optimization modeling language. It is designed to define optimization problems and solve them with various solvers like CBC, Gurobi, and GLPK.

   o **Pulp:** A linear programming library that provides a simple way to define linear and mixed-integer optimization problems.

Real-World Example: Optimizing Material Usage in Structural Engineering

Optimization plays a crucial role in structural engineering, particularly in optimizing material usage while maintaining the structural integrity of a design. A common problem is minimizing the amount of material used in a structural component (such as beams, columns, or trusses) while ensuring it can withstand the required loads.

Let's say you're designing a beam and want to minimize its weight (and therefore its material usage), subject to the constraint that it must support a certain load without bending or breaking.

To simplify the problem, let's consider a one-dimensional beam with the following parameters:

- **Length of the beam:** L (meters)
- **Material density:** ρ (kg/m³)
- **Cross-sectional area:** A (m²)
- **Young's Modulus (E):** A measure of material stiffness
- **Force (F):** Applied load (N)

The objective is to minimize the material used, which is proportional to the cross-sectional area A, subject to the constraint that the beam must support the load without exceeding a certain deflection δ_max.

The deflection δ of a beam can be calculated using the formula:

$\delta = F \cdot L33 \cdot E \cdot I \backslash delta = \backslash frac\{F \backslash cdot L^3\}\{3 \backslash cdot E \backslash cdot I\} \delta = 3 \cdot E \cdot IF \cdot L3$

Where I is the moment of inertia of the beam's cross-section, and it depends on the geometry of the beam. In this case, let's assume the beam has a rectangular cross-section, so:

$I = A212I = \backslash frac\{A^2\}\{12\}I = 12A2$

Now, we want to minimize the cross-sectional area A while ensuring that the deflection δ does not exceed a specified limit.

Here's how this problem might look in Python using SciPy:

python

```
import numpy as np
from scipy.optimize import minimize

# Constants
L = 10  # Length of the beam (meters)
F = 1000  # Applied force (Newtons)
E = 2.1e11  # Young's Modulus for steel (Pa)
delta_max = 0.01  # Maximum allowable deflection (meters)

# Objective function: Minimize the cross-sectional area A
def objective(A):
    return A  # Minimize area, i.e., material usage

# Constraint: Deflection must not exceed delta_max
def constraint(A):
```

```
I = A**2 / 12  # Moment of inertia for rectangular cross-section
delta = (F * L**3) / (3 * E * I)
return delta_max - delta  # The difference should be >= 0


# Initial guess for cross-sectional area
A0 = 0.1


# Define the constraint
cons = {'type': 'ineq', 'fun': constraint}


# Solve the optimization problem
result = minimize(objective, A0, constraints=cons)


print("Optimal cross-sectional area (m²):", result.x[0])
```

In this example, we use SciPy to minimize the material used in the beam while ensuring that the deflection does not exceed the allowable limit. The output will provide the optimal cross-sectional area required to support the load.

Optimization is an essential tool in engineering design, and Python provides powerful libraries and frameworks to solve optimization problems. By using SciPy, CVXPY, and other optimization libraries, engineers can optimize designs in various fields, such as structural engineering, mechanical systems, and even software engineering. In this chapter, we've covered basic optimization principles, introduced Python solvers, and walked through a real-world example in structural engineering to demonstrate the practical application of optimization techniques.

As you continue to explore Python for engineering, optimization will remain a fundamental tool to enhance your ability to solve complex engineering problems efficiently and effectively.

Chapter 9: Automation in Engineering – Automating Repetitive Tasks

In the world of engineering, time is a precious commodity, and engineers are often tasked with repetitive and time-consuming processes such as data analysis, simulation runs, and report generation. Python is a powerful tool for automating these processes, significantly enhancing productivity and allowing engineers to focus on higher-level problem-solving and decision-making. This chapter will cover the basics of using Python for task automation, specifically in engineering contexts, and will include real-world examples of automating repetitive engineering tasks.

Using Python for Task Automation

Automation in engineering often involves using Python to eliminate manual intervention in repetitive tasks. These tasks may range from simple calculations to complex simulation workflows or even entire data processing pipelines. Automation reduces the risk of human error, speeds up tasks, and ensures consistency across multiple iterations.

1. Automating Repetitive Engineering Calculations

In many engineering fields, calculations such as determining stress, load, or efficiency are required repeatedly across a wide range of projects or simulations. Instead of manually entering data and running calculations every time, Python can help by creating scripts that automatically perform these calculations.

Example: Calculating Structural Load

Consider a scenario where an engineer needs to calculate the structural load on a series of beams repeatedly. Instead of manually plugging in values for each beam, Python can be used to automate the calculation.

python

```python
def calculate_load(force, area):
    # Calculate stress (Force / Area)
    return force / area


# List of beam forces and areas
beam_data = [(5000, 10), (7500, 12), (10000, 15)]


# Calculate the stress for each beam
for force, area in beam_data:
    stress = calculate_load(force, area)
    print(f"Stress on beam with force {force}N and area {area}m^2: {stress} Pa")
```

This script automates the repetitive task of calculating the stress for different beams, providing quick and accurate results.

2. Automating Simulations and Modeling

Many engineering applications require running simulations, whether for structural analysis, fluid dynamics, or thermal systems.

These simulations often need to be run under various conditions, with different input parameters, creating a large number of repetitive tasks.

Python can automate the setup, execution, and logging of these simulations. For example, using Python in combination with tools like ANSYS or COMSOL (via their APIs), engineers can automatically set simulation parameters, run the simulations, and collect results.

python

```python
import os

def run_simulation(parameter_set):
    # Simulate running an engineering model (simplified)
    os.system(f"run_simulation --param {parameter_set}")

# Automate running multiple simulations
parameter_sets = ['param1', 'param2', 'param3']
for param in parameter_sets:
    run_simulation(param)
```

This way, engineers can batch-run simulations with different parameters, saving significant time.

Real-World Example: Automating Data Collection from Sensors and Saving Results to Files

Another common engineering task is collecting data from various sensors (e.g., temperature, pressure, vibration) and saving that data for analysis or reporting. This task is particularly relevant in fields like mechanical and civil engineering, where continuous monitoring of systems is essential.

Python's libraries like time, os, and pySerial (for serial communication) can be used to automate the process of reading sensor data and saving it to files such as CSV or Excel.

Example: Collecting Data from a Temperature Sensor

python

```python
import time
import csv


def read_sensor_data():
    # Simulating reading data from a sensor (e.g., temperature)
    temperature = 25.0 + (0.5 * time.time() % 5)  # Simulated sensor data
    return temperature


# Automate data collection every second and save to a CSV file
def collect_and_save_data(duration=10):
    with open("sensor_data.csv", mode='w', newline='') as file:
        writer = csv.writer(file)
        writer.writerow(["Time (s)", "Temperature (C)"])  # Writing header
        start_time = time.time()
        while time.time() - start_time < duration:
            sensor_data = read_sensor_data()
            writer.writerow([time.time() - start_time, sensor_data])
            time.sleep(1)  # Collect data every second
```

```
# Collect data for 10 seconds
collect_and_save_data()
```

In this example, the script automates the process of reading data from a simulated temperature sensor every second and stores it in a CSV file. The engineer does not have to manually collect the data; the script takes care of it, allowing the engineer to focus on the analysis.

Why Automation is Crucial in Engineering

Automation brings several benefits to engineering tasks, including:

1. **Time-Saving:** Tasks that would take hours or even days can be completed in seconds or minutes, freeing up time for engineers to focus on more complex problems.
2. **Error Reduction:** Automation minimizes the possibility of human error, ensuring that calculations, simulations, or data collection are done consistently and accurately.
3. **Scalability:** With automation, tasks can be scaled up easily. For example, running hundreds of simulations or collecting data from thousands of sensors becomes feasible without human intervention.
4. **Reproducibility:** Automated processes ensure that experiments, simulations, or calculations are done exactly the same way each time, which is crucial for engineering analysis.

Next Steps: Expanding Automation in Engineering

As engineers become more proficient in Python, they can begin to explore more advanced automation tasks, such as:

- **Automating the entire design pipeline:** From initial design sketches to final simulations and material procurement.
- **Integrating with other software tools:** Automating tasks across different engineering tools (e.g., CAD software, finite element analysis tools).
- **Setting up real-time monitoring systems:** Automating the monitoring of engineering systems, from live sensor data collection to alerting engineers when certain thresholds are exceeded.

By leveraging Python's simplicity and versatility, engineers can dramatically increase their efficiency and accuracy, automating countless aspects of their daily tasks.

Automation is one of Python's greatest strengths in engineering applications. With just a few lines of code, engineers can automate repetitive calculations, simulations, and data collection tasks, saving valuable time and ensuring consistency. By following the examples in this chapter and exploring more advanced techniques, engineers can optimize their workflows and focus their efforts on solving more complex engineering challenges.

Chapter 10: Simulation Modeling in Engineering with Python

Simulation plays a critical role in modern engineering. It allows engineers to model and analyze complex physical systems that would be difficult or impossible to study through direct experimentation. Python, with its rich ecosystem of libraries, offers a powerful platform for creating simulation models across various engineering domains such as mechanical, electrical, fluid dynamics, and more. This chapter explores how Python can be used to model and simulate engineering systems, with a focus on building a simulation for electrical circuit analysis.

Introduction to Simulation in Engineering

Simulations in engineering are used to replicate the behavior of real-world systems by creating a virtual model of the system. These models can simulate everything from the mechanical behavior of structures under load to the behavior of electrical circuits under varying conditions. Simulation provides engineers with insights into how a system will behave in real-world scenarios, often leading to better designs, optimization, and safety analyses.

1. Simulating Physical Systems

Simulation models in engineering can be broadly classified into the following categories:

- **Mechanical Systems**: Simulating mechanical systems often involves solving differential equations that describe the motion, forces, and stresses within a system. Applications include structural analysis, stress testing, vibration analysis, and thermal systems.

- **Electrical Systems**: Simulating electrical circuits allows engineers to predict the behavior of circuits, such as voltage, current, and power flow under different conditions. Simulation models are crucial for designing efficient and reliable circuits without the need for physical prototypes.

- **Fluid Dynamics**: Fluid dynamics simulations are used to model the flow of liquids and gases. These models can be complex, involving computational fluid dynamics (CFD) to predict the behavior of fluids under various conditions, such as pressure changes, temperature variations, or airflow across surfaces.

- **Control Systems**: In control engineering, simulations are used to model dynamic systems and control mechanisms. This includes everything from automated systems to robotics and manufacturing lines.

2. Simulation in Electrical Engineering

In electrical engineering, simulation is used to design and test circuits, analyze performance, and predict how components will behave when exposed to different electrical signals or configurations. This includes everything from simple resistive circuits to complex power distribution systems.

Some common techniques used in electrical circuit simulations include:

- **SPICE (Simulation Program with Integrated Circuit Emphasis)**: A tool that is widely used for simulating electronic circuits.
- **Finite Element Method (FEM)**: A numerical method used for solving partial differential equations, often used in electromagnetic field simulations.

However, Python can provide a more accessible and customizable platform for engineers who want to implement simulations without relying on specialized software.

Real-World Example: Building a Simulation Model for Electrical Circuit Analysis

One of the most common tasks in electrical engineering is analyzing circuits to determine the relationship between voltage, current, and resistance. Ohm's Law ($V = IR$) is a fundamental equation in circuit analysis, but real-world circuits are often more complex, involving multiple components such as resistors, capacitors, inductors, and voltage sources. In this example, we will build a Python model to simulate a simple electrical circuit containing a resistor and capacitor in series.

Step 1: Setting Up the Problem

Let's model a series RC circuit where we have:

- A **resistor (R)** with a resistance of $1k\Omega$
- A **capacitor (C)** with a capacitance of $1\mu F$
- A **DC voltage source (V)** providing 5V.

The goal is to calculate the voltage across the capacitor over time as it charges, given that the initial voltage across the capacitor is zero.

Step 2: Implementing the Simulation in Python

To simulate this circuit, we can use Python to numerically solve the differential equation that governs the charging process of the capacitor. The equation for a charging capacitor in an RC circuit is:

$$VC(t)=V(1-e-t/(R*C))V\_C(t) = V(1 - e^{\{-t / (R * C)\}})VC(t)=V(1-e-t/(R*C))$$

Where:

- $VC(t)V\_C(t)VC(t)$ is the voltage across the capacitor at time ttt,
- VVV is the supply voltage,
- RRR is the resistance,
- CCC is the capacitance,
- eee is the base of the natural logarithm.

We can use NumPy to implement the time-stepping procedure and Matplotlib for plotting the results.

Step 3: Writing the Python Code

python

```python
import numpy as np
import matplotlib.pyplot as plt

# Given values
V = 5  # Supply voltage in volts
R = 1e3  # Resistance in ohms (1 kΩ)
C = 1e-6  # Capacitance in farads (1 µF)

# Time array from 0 to 5 seconds
t = np.linspace(0, 5, 1000)

# Voltage across the capacitor at each time step
V_C = V * (1 - np.exp(-t / (R * C)))

# Plotting the voltage across the capacitor
plt.plot(t, V_C)
plt.title('Charging of a Capacitor in an RC Circuit')
plt.xlabel('Time (seconds)')
plt.ylabel('Voltage Across Capacitor (V)')
plt.grid(True)
plt.show()
```

Step 4: Understanding the Results

In this simulation, we calculated the voltage across the capacitor at various time intervals and plotted the result. The plot will show the voltage increasing exponentially over time, approaching the supply voltage of 5V as time progresses. This is characteristic of the charging curve of a capacitor in an RC circuit.

- Initially, the voltage is low, as the capacitor is not charged.
- Over time, the voltage increases, but it slows down as the capacitor approaches its maximum charge.
- Eventually, the voltage across the capacitor asymptotically approaches 5V.

Enhancing the Simulation

For a more advanced simulation, engineers can include additional elements such as:

- **Voltage sources** with varying signals (AC or pulsed).
- **Multiple components** such as resistors, inductors, or additional capacitors to simulate more complex circuits.
- **Time-domain analysis** to observe the system's response over extended periods.

Real-World Applications and Further Exploration

While this example focuses on a simple RC circuit, Python simulations can be applied to a wide variety of electrical engineering problems:

- **AC Circuits**: Analyzing alternating current (AC) circuits by solving complex differential equations.

- **Power Systems**: Simulating electrical grids to optimize power distribution.

- **Signal Processing**: Simulating filters, amplifiers, and other electronic components used in signal processing.

- **Control Systems**: Modeling control loops and response behaviors for system stability analysis.

By applying simulation modeling in Python, engineers can save time, reduce errors, and gain deeper insights into the behavior of their designs before implementing physical prototypes.

In this chapter, we have explored how Python can be used to simulate engineering systems, with a focus on electrical circuit analysis. By leveraging Python's libraries like NumPy and SciPy, engineers can easily create simulation models that solve complex equations, automate repetitive tasks, and visualize results in meaningful ways. This chapter provided a hands-on example of simulating an RC circuit, but the techniques discussed can be applied to a wide range of engineering problems across various disciplines.

Chapter 11: Signal Processing in Engineering with Python

Signal processing is a crucial aspect of engineering, particularly in fields such as electrical engineering, mechanical systems, communications, and more. With Python's extensive libraries and robust mathematical capabilities, engineers can efficiently process and analyze signals, whether they come from sensors, microphones, or other sources. This chapter delves into the basics of signal processing, focusing on how Python tools like NumPy and SciPy can be utilized to perform operations like Fourier transforms, filtering, and data analysis. The chapter will also walk through a real-world example of processing sensor data in mechanical engineering applications.

Introduction to Signal Processing

Signal processing refers to the manipulation, analysis, and interpretation of signals, which can include sound, electrical signals, or mechanical vibrations. In many engineering applications, signals are often noisy and need to be filtered, transformed, or analyzed for specific characteristics such as frequency components, amplitude, or phase. Signal processing can be categorized into two main types:

1. **Analog Signal Processing**: Dealing with continuous signals, typically handled using hardware such as filters or amplifiers.

2. **Digital Signal Processing (DSP)**: Working with discrete signals, which involves algorithms and computation. Python, through libraries like SciPy and NumPy, excels in digital signal processing tasks.

Python provides engineers with powerful libraries and tools that make the implementation of signal processing tasks simpler and more accessible. NumPy, for instance, provides support for large, multi-dimensional arrays and matrices, along with a collection of mathematical functions to operate on these arrays. SciPy builds upon this with additional functionality, specifically for more advanced mathematical and signal processing operations.

Using Python for Signal Processing in Electrical and Mechanical Engineering

Python's flexibility in handling numerical and matrix operations makes it a go-to language for signal processing tasks in engineering. Whether you're working on processing data from an accelerometer in mechanical systems, analyzing electrical waveforms, or filtering audio signals, Python offers tools that simplify the process.

1. **Fourier Transform**: The Fourier Transform is a mathematical technique that breaks down complex signals into their constituent frequencies. In signal processing, this is commonly used for analyzing signals in the frequency domain. Python's numpy.fft module allows for quick and efficient Fast Fourier Transforms (FFT), a crucial tool for engineers working in fields like acoustics or vibrations analysis.

2. **Filtering**: Filtering is used to remove unwanted noise from signals. Python's scipy.signal module provides a range of functions for filtering data, such as low-pass, high-pass, and band-pass filters. Engineers can use these functions to design filters that isolate certain frequency ranges, which is essential when working with real-world signals that often contain noise or irrelevant information.

3. **Windowing Functions**: In signal processing, windowing functions are used to isolate a portion of the signal for analysis. Common windows include Hamming, Hanning, and Blackman-Harris, all of which are available in Python via the scipy.signal library.

4. **Data Transformation and Analysis**: In mechanical systems, engineers often need to analyze data from sensors that measure vibrations, acceleration, and pressure. With tools like NumPy, Python allows for easy manipulation and

analysis of sensor data, such as finding the peaks, calculating averages, or detecting anomalies.

Tools: SciPy and NumPy for Fourier Transforms, Filters

1. **SciPy**: The scipy.signal module in SciPy provides powerful tools for signal processing, including functions for filtering, convolution, and spectral analysis. For instance, functions like scipy.signal.firwin allow for the creation of finite impulse response (FIR) filters, and scipy.signal.welch provides tools for power spectral density estimation.

2. **NumPy**: The numpy.fft module in NumPy provides a straightforward interface for performing Fast Fourier Transforms. It's commonly used for converting a signal from the time domain into the frequency domain, allowing engineers to analyze the signal's frequency components.

3. **Matplotlib**: For visualization, matplotlib is an essential tool. It allows engineers to plot signals in both the time and frequency domains, making it easier to interpret the data and identify patterns.

Real-World Example: Processing Signals from an Accelerometer or Microphone

In mechanical systems, accelerometers are often used to measure vibrations or movements of components, and microphones are used to capture sound or vibrations. For this example, we will simulate processing accelerometer data in Python to identify frequency components and apply filters to clean up the signal.

Let's assume you are working with data from an accelerometer that measures the vibration of a machine part. The goal is to process the raw signal, remove noise, and identify the dominant frequency of vibration.

1. **Simulating Accelerometer Data**: You will start by simulating accelerometer data that includes noise and a known signal of interest.

python

```
import numpy as np
import matplotlib.pyplot as plt

# Sampling parameters
fs = 1000  # Sampling frequency (Hz)
t = np.linspace(0, 1, fs)  # 1 second of data

# Simulating a noisy accelerometer signal with a known frequency
signal_freq = 50  # Signal frequency in Hz
noise = np.random.normal(0, 0.5, fs)  # Random noise
signal = np.sin(2 * np.pi * signal_freq * t)  # Sine wave signal

accelerometer_data = signal + noise

# Plotting the raw signal
```

```
plt.plot(t, accelerometer_data)
plt.title("Raw Accelerometer Signal")
plt.xlabel("Time (s)")
plt.ylabel("Acceleration (m/s^2)")
plt.show()
```

2. **Fourier Transform to Identify Frequency Components**:
   The next step is to apply a Fourier Transform to analyze the
   frequency content of the accelerometer data. This will
   allow you to identify the dominant frequencies in the signal.

   python

```
from scipy.fft import fft, fftfreq

# Perform Fast Fourier Transform (FFT)
N = len(accelerometer_data)
freqs = fftfreq(N, 1/fs)
fft_values = fft(accelerometer_data)

# Plotting the frequency spectrum
plt.plot(freqs[:N//2], np.abs(fft_values)[:N//2])
plt.title("Frequency Spectrum of Accelerometer Signal")
plt.xlabel("Frequency (Hz)")
plt.ylabel("Amplitude")
plt.show()
```

The Fourier Transform will reveal the dominant
frequencies present in the accelerometer signal. In this case,
we should expect to see a peak around 50 Hz, which

corresponds to the known frequency of the machine's vibration.

3. **Filtering Noise**: Next, we will filter out the noise from the signal using a low-pass filter. This will allow us to isolate the frequency of interest (50 Hz) and remove higher frequency noise.

python

```python
from scipy.signal import butter, filtfilt

# Design a low-pass filter with a cutoff frequency of 60 Hz
def butter_lowpass(cutoff, fs, order=4):
    nyquist = 0.5 * fs
    normal_cutoff = cutoff / nyquist
    b, a = butter(order, normal_cutoff, btype='low', analog=False)
    return b, a

# Apply the filter to the signal
b, a = butter_lowpass(60, fs, order=4)
filtered_signal = filtfilt(b, a, accelerometer_data)

# Plot the filtered signal
plt.plot(t, filtered_signal)
plt.title("Filtered Accelerometer Signal")
plt.xlabel("Time (s)")
plt.ylabel("Acceleration (m/s^2)")
plt.show()
```

This real-world example demonstrates how Python, with its powerful signal processing libraries, can be used to analyze and filter accelerometer data in mechanical systems. By applying Fourier Transforms, filtering, and visualization techniques, engineers can gain valuable insights into the behavior of physical systems.

Signal processing is a powerful tool for engineers, and Python makes it accessible for a wide range of applications. Whether it's analyzing vibration data in mechanical systems or processing audio signals in electrical engineering, Python's capabilities through libraries like SciPy, NumPy, and Matplotlib are indispensable. Engineers can apply these tools to improve the accuracy of their analyses, design better systems, and automate repetitive tasks, all of which ultimately lead to better, more efficient engineering solutions.

Chapter 12: Control Systems – Modeling and Simulation

Control systems are fundamental to many engineering disciplines, including mechanical, electrical, aerospace, and industrial engineering. These systems regulate the behavior of a process to maintain desired outputs despite disturbances. Common applications include regulating the speed of motors, the temperature in a heating system, or the position of an object in robotics. In this chapter, we will explore how Python can be used to model and simulate control systems, focusing on the use of tools like NumPy and SciPy to implement key concepts such as PID controllers, transfer functions, and system dynamics.

Introduction to Control Systems

A control system uses feedback to control the behavior of a dynamic system. The goal is to ensure that the system performs as desired by regulating its outputs, such as temperature, speed, or position. Control systems can be broadly classified into:

1. **Open-Loop Control Systems**: Systems that do not use feedback to adjust their operation. For example, a washing machine that runs for a fixed time without measuring the cleanliness of clothes.

2. **Closed-Loop Control Systems**: Systems that use feedback to adjust their operation. The most common type of closed-

loop control system is the **feedback control system**, where a sensor measures the output, compares it to the desired setpoint, and adjusts the control input to bring the system closer to the desired state.

Python's powerful libraries, such as **NumPy** and **SciPy**, make it ideal for modeling and simulating these systems.

Control System Components

A control system typically consists of several key components:

1. **Controller**: The part of the system that adjusts the input based on feedback from the process. Common controllers include **Proportional-Integral-Derivative (PID)** controllers, **Lead-Lag controllers**, and **State-space controllers**.
2. **Process**: The system being controlled, such as a motor, temperature regulator, or robot arm.
3. **Sensor**: A device that measures the output of the process, providing feedback to the controller.
4. **Actuator**: A device that alters the process's state based on the controller's commands.

Modeling Control Systems with Python

Python allows engineers to model control systems using mathematical techniques. To simulate control systems, we often use **transfer functions** and **state-space representations** of systems, which describe the relationship between input and output. For time-domain simulation, **differential equations** are solved to observe how the system behaves over time.

Step 1: Modeling a System with Transfer Functions

A **transfer function** describes the input-output relationship of a linear time-invariant system. It is typically expressed as the ratio of the Laplace transform of the output to the Laplace transform of the input.

In Python, the **control** library provides tools for working with transfer functions and performing system analysis.

python

```
import numpy as np
import matplotlib.pyplot as plt
import control as ctrl

# Define the system: transfer function H(s) = 1 / (s + 1)
numerator = [1]
denominator = [1, 1]  # s + 1
system = ctrl.TransferFunction(numerator, denominator)

# Time array for simulation
time = np.linspace(0, 10, 1000)

# Generate a step input signal
time, output = ctrl.step_response(system, time)
```

```
# Plot the output response
plt.plot(time, output)
plt.title("Step Response of the System")
plt.xlabel("Time (s)")
plt.ylabel("Output")
plt.grid(True)
plt.show()
```

In this example, we simulate the step response of a simple first-order system with the transfer function $H(s)=1s+1H(s)$ = \frac{1}{s+1}$H(s)=s+11$, where sss is the Laplace operator.

Step 2: Implementing a PID Controller

A **PID controller** is one of the most widely used controllers in engineering. It adjusts the control signal based on three components:

1. **Proportional (P)**: Corrects the error proportionally to its magnitude.
2. **Integral (I)**: Corrects accumulated errors over time.
3. **Derivative (D)**: Corrects based on the rate of change of the error.

The PID controller is typically defined as:

$C(s)=Kp+Kis+Kd\cdot sC(s)$ = K_p + \frac{K_i}{s}$ + $K\_d \cdot s$ $C(s)=Kp+sKi+Kd\cdot s$

Where KpK_pKp, KiK_iKi, and KdK_dKd are the proportional, integral, and derivative gains, respectively.

Step 3: Tuning the PID Controller

Tuning the PID controller involves adjusting KpK_pKp, KiK_iKi, and KdK_dKd to achieve the desired system response. This can be done manually or using optimization techniques, such as the Ziegler-Nichols method or trial and error.

python

```python
# Define PID parameters
Kp = 2.0  # Proportional gain
Ki = 0.5  # Integral gain
Kd = 1.0  # Derivative gain

# Define the PID controller
pid_controller = ctrl.TransferFunction([Kd, Kp, Ki], [1, 0])

# Closed-loop system: G(s) / (1 + G(s) * H(s))
closed_loop_system = ctrl.feedback(pid_controller * system, 1)

# Simulate the response to a step input
time, response = ctrl.step_response(closed_loop_system, time)

# Plot the closed-loop response
plt.plot(time, response)
plt.title("Closed-Loop Step Response with PID Controller")
plt.xlabel("Time (s)")
plt.ylabel("Output")
plt.grid(True)
plt.show()
```

This code defines a simple PID controller, simulates the closed-loop response of the system, and visualizes how the system behaves after applying feedback.

Real-World Example: Simulating the Behavior of a PID Controller

To understand the real-world applications of control systems, let's consider the simulation of a **PID controller** used to regulate the **temperature** of an industrial furnace.

Problem Setup

In this example, we will simulate the temperature regulation of a furnace. The furnace has a heating element that increases the temperature, and a cooling element that reduces it. The system uses a PID controller to adjust the heating and cooling rates to maintain a setpoint temperature despite external disturbances.

Step 1: Modeling the Furnace System

We can model the furnace using a simple first-order system that responds to changes in the heating and cooling inputs.

python

```
# Define a simple furnace model as a transfer function
furnace_system = ctrl.TransferFunction([1], [10, 1])  # simple first-order system
```

Step 2: Implementing the PID Controller

Next, we will apply a PID controller to regulate the temperature.

python

```
# Define PID controller for temperature regulation
Kp_temp = 2.5
Ki_temp = 0.1
Kd_temp = 1.0

pid_temp_controller = ctrl.TransferFunction([Kd_temp, Kp_temp, Ki_temp], [1, 0])

# Create a closed-loop system for the temperature regulation
closed_loop_temp_system    =    ctrl.feedback(pid_temp_controller    *
furnace_system, 1)
```

Step 3: Simulating the Temperature Response

Finally, we simulate the system's response to a setpoint change and visualize the results.

python

```
# Simulate the closed-loop system's response to a step input (setpoint change)
time, temperature_response = ctrl.step_response(closed_loop_temp_system, time)

# Plot the temperature response
plt.plot(time, temperature_response)
plt.title("Furnace Temperature Control with PID")
plt.xlabel("Time (s)")
plt.ylabel("Temperature (°C)")
plt.grid(True)
plt.show()
```

This example simulates the closed-loop response of a furnace temperature control system using a PID controller. The result is a smooth temperature regulation that minimizes overshoot and settling time.

Python is a powerful tool for modeling and simulating control systems. With libraries such as **NumPy**, **SciPy**, and **control**, engineers can model dynamic systems, design controllers, and simulate their behavior efficiently. The PID controller example demonstrates the application of control theory in a real-world engineering scenario, showing how Python can help solve complex engineering problems.

In the next chapter, we will explore more advanced control strategies and dive deeper into state-space modeling and optimal control systems.

Chapter 13: Structural Engineering – Analyzing and Modeling Structures

Structural engineering plays a pivotal role in ensuring the safety, stability, and durability of buildings, bridges, dams, and other infrastructure. Python, with its powerful libraries and frameworks, offers engineers an excellent tool to perform complex calculations, simulations, and analyses that were traditionally handled by specialized software. In this chapter, we will explore how Python can be applied in structural analysis, particularly focusing on Finite Element Analysis (FEA), a common method for simulating how structures respond to forces, and other key tasks in structural engineering.

Using Python for Structural Analysis

Structural analysis involves evaluating the strength, stability, and load-bearing capacity of structures. Engineers use a range of methods and tools to simulate forces acting on a structure and predict its response. In recent years, Python has become a popular tool for structural analysis due to its flexibility, ease of use, and the availability of libraries for numerical computation, data handling, and visualization.

1. Finite Element Analysis (FEA)

FEA is a computational method used to predict how a structure behaves under various physical conditions such as loads, heat, vibrations, and stresses. It divides a large system into smaller, simpler parts called "finite elements," which are analyzed individually. These elements are then recombined to give an overall solution for the entire system.

In the context of Python, several libraries can help with performing FEA, including **NumPy** (for numerical calculations), **SciPy** (for optimization and numerical methods), and **PyFEM** or **FEniCS** (specific libraries for finite element simulations).

Key steps in an FEA process include:

1. **Mesh Generation**: Dividing the structure into smaller elements (meshing).
2. **Defining Material Properties**: Defining the materials (e.g., steel, concrete) and their physical properties (e.g., Young's Modulus, Poisson's Ratio).
3. **Boundary Conditions**: Applying constraints and loads to the structure, such as fixed points or applied forces.
4. **Solving the System of Equations**: Using numerical methods to solve the resulting system of equations.
5. **Post-Processing**: Analyzing and visualizing the results to understand how the structure behaves under different loading conditions.

2. Python Libraries for Structural Analysis

- **NumPy and SciPy**: These libraries provide essential tools for performing matrix operations and solving the system of equations that arise from FEA. They also support linear algebra operations, optimization, and integration, all of which are important in structural analysis.
- **PyFEM**: A Python library for finite element modeling that enables users to create, solve, and analyze FEA problems.
- **FEniCS**: An open-source computing platform for solving partial differential equations (PDEs) using finite element methods. It is widely used for structural simulations in engineering.
- **Matplotlib and Seaborn**: These libraries help with visualizing the results of FEA simulations, such as stress distribution or displacement maps.

Real-World Example: Analyzing the Stress Distribution in a Beam Using Python

To illustrate how Python can be used in structural analysis, we will work through a simple example: analyzing the stress distribution in a cantilever beam under a uniform load. The problem setup and the necessary steps will be as follows:

Problem Setup:

We are tasked with analyzing a cantilever beam subjected to a uniformly distributed load. The goal is to calculate the stress distribution along the length of the beam.

- **Beam Properties**:
  - Length: 10 meters
  - Young's Modulus (E): 200 GPa (Gigapascals)
  - Moment of Inertia (I): 5000 cm^4
  - Uniform Load: 500 N/m

We need to calculate the stress at different points along the beam.

Step 1: Defining the Parameters

We start by importing the necessary libraries and defining the problem parameters:

python

```
import numpy as np
import matplotlib.pyplot as plt


# Beam properties
length = 10  # Length of the beam in meters
E = 200e9  # Young's Modulus in Pascals
I = 5000e-8  # Moment of inertia in m^4
w = 500  # Uniform load in N/m


# Discretizing the beam into 100 points
x = np.linspace(0, length, 100)
```

Step 2: Calculating the Bending Moment

The bending moment at any point x along the beam under a uniform load is given by the equation:

$M(x)=w2\cdot(L-x)\cdot xM(x) = \frac{w}{2} \cdot (L - x) \cdot xM(x)=2w\cdot(L-x)\cdot x$

Where w is the uniform load, L is the length of the beam, and x is the distance from the fixed end of the beam.

python

```
# Calculating the bending moment at each point along the beam
M = (w / 2) * (length - x) * x
```

Step 3: Calculating the Stress

The stress at any point along the beam due to bending is given by the formula:

$\sigma(x)=M(x)I\sigma(x) = \frac{M(x)}{I}\sigma(x)=IM(x)$

Where $M(x)$ is the bending moment and I is the moment of inertia.

python

```
# Calculating the stress at each point along the beam
stress = M / I
```

Step 4: Visualizing the Stress Distribution

We now visualize the stress distribution along the beam using a simple plot:

python

```
# Plotting the stress distribution
```

```
plt.plot(x, stress, label="Stress Distribution")
plt.title("Stress Distribution in a Cantilever Beam")
plt.xlabel("Position along the Beam (m)")
plt.ylabel("Stress (Pa)")
plt.legend()
plt.grid(True)
plt.show()
```

This plot will show how the stress varies along the length of the beam, with maximum stress occurring at the fixed end.

Python provides a flexible and powerful platform for performing structural analysis and modeling. By leveraging libraries like NumPy, SciPy, and specialized tools such as PyFEM and FEniCS, engineers can simulate real-world systems and analyze the behavior of structures under different conditions. In this chapter, we demonstrated how Python can be used to perform a basic structural analysis—calculating the stress distribution along a cantilever beam—using numerical methods and visualization techniques.

By applying similar techniques, engineers can extend this approach to more complex structures and simulations, including multi-dimensional analyses and dynamic systems, allowing for better-informed decision-making in engineering design and safety.

Chapter 14: Electrical Engineering – Circuit Simulation

Electrical engineering involves the design, analysis, and optimization of electrical systems, from simple circuits to complex systems powering entire industries. Python has emerged as an incredibly powerful tool for modeling and simulating electrical circuits, offering engineers a versatile and cost-effective alternative to proprietary simulation software. In this chapter, we will focus on using Python for circuit simulation, covering how to model electrical components, simulate circuits, and perform analysis of key electrical parameters such as voltage, current, and power.

Modeling Electrical Circuits in Python

Python allows engineers to create models of electrical circuits, from simple resistor-capacitor (RC) circuits to more complex systems involving resistors, inductors, and capacitors (RLC circuits). By combining Python's rich ecosystem of scientific libraries with its flexibility and ease of use, electrical engineers can simulate circuits, perform dynamic analysis, and visualize results to gain insights into their systems.

1. Understanding RLC Circuits and Circuit Analysis

An RLC circuit consists of a resistor (R), an inductor (L), and a capacitor (C) connected in series or parallel. RLC circuits are fundamental to many electrical systems, including oscillators, filters, and power distribution networks. To analyze such circuits, engineers often use differential equations that describe the behavior of the components in the circuit.

- **Resistor (R)**: Resists the flow of current, with a voltage drop proportional to the current.
- **Inductor (L)**: Stores energy in a magnetic field and resists changes in current.
- **Capacitor (C)**: Stores energy in an electric field and resists changes in voltage.

The behavior of an RLC circuit can be described using Kirchhoff's voltage law (KVL) and Kirchhoff's current law (KCL). These laws are expressed in the form of differential equations that describe how the voltage and current vary over time.

In Python, the most common way to solve these equations is using numerical integration methods, such as Euler's method or Runge-Kutta methods, which allow us to simulate the behavior of the circuit over time.

2. Python Libraries for Circuit Simulation

Several Python libraries can be used to model and simulate electrical circuits, including:

- **SciPy**: Offers tools for solving ordinary differential equations (ODEs) and numerical integration, essential for solving circuit equations.
- **NumPy**: Provides support for efficient numerical computations, such as matrix operations, which are crucial for analyzing complex circuits.
- **PySpice**: A Python interface for the popular SPICE (Simulation Program with Integrated Circuit Emphasis) engine, which allows engineers to simulate analog electronic circuits.

3. Simulating an RLC Circuit in Python

Let's simulate a simple RLC circuit in Python using SciPy for numerical integration. We'll simulate a series RLC circuit and calculate the current over time for different values of resistance, inductance, and capacitance.

Step 1: Define the Circuit Parameters

In an RLC circuit, the differential equation governing the circuit can be written as:

Ld2i(t)dt2+Rdi(t)dt+1Ci(t)=V(t)L   \frac{d^2i(t)}{dt^2}   +   R \frac{di(t)}{dt} + \frac{1}{C} i(t) = V(t)Ldt2d2i(t)+Rdtdi(t)+C1 i(t)=V(t)

Where:

- $i(t)i(t)i(t)$ is the current as a function of time.
- RRR is the resistance in ohms.
- LLL is the inductance in henries.
- CCC is the capacitance in farads.
- $V(t)V(t)V(t)$ is the input voltage (which can be a constant or time-varying function).

Step 2: Define the Differential Equations

To solve the differential equation, we first need to convert it into a system of first-order differential equations. This can be done by defining the current $i(t)i(t)i(t)$ and the voltage across the inductor $vL(t)v\_L(t)vL(t)$ as state variables.

di(t)dt=vL(t)\frac{di(t)}{dt} $=$ v_L(t)dtdi(t)=vL(t) dvL(t)dt=V(t)−Ri(t)−1Ci(t)L\frac{dv_L(t)}{dt} = \frac{V(t) - R i(t) - \frac{1}{C} i(t)}{L}dtdvL(t)=LV(t)−Ri(t)−C1i(t)

Step 3: Code the Simulation in Python

Let's implement this system of differential equations using Python's SciPy library.

python

```
import numpy as np
import scipy.integrate as integrate
import matplotlib.pyplot as plt
```

```python
# Circuit parameters
R = 1.0  # Resistance (Ohms)
L = 1.0  # Inductance (Henries)
C = 1.0  # Capacitance (Farads)
V = 1.0  # Input Voltage (Volts)

# Define the differential equations
def rlc_circuit(t, y):
    i, v_L = y
    di_dt = v_L
    dv_L_dt = (V - R*i - (1/C)*i) / L
    return [di_dt, dv_L_dt]

# Initial conditions: initial current and voltage across the inductor
y0 = [0, 0]  # Initially no current and no voltage

# Time vector for simulation
t = np.linspace(0, 10, 1000)  # Simulate from t=0 to t=10 seconds

# Solve the differential equations
solution = integrate.odeint(rlc_circuit, y0, t)

# Extract the current and voltage
current = solution[:, 0]
voltage_L = solution[:, 1]

# Plot the results
plt.figure(figsize=(10, 6))
plt.subplot(2, 1, 1)
plt.plot(t, current, label='Current (i(t))', color='b')
```

```
plt.xlabel('Time (s)')
plt.ylabel('Current (A)')
plt.title('Current in Series RLC Circuit')
plt.legend()

plt.subplot(2, 1, 2)
plt.plot(t, voltage_L, label='Voltage across Inductor (v_L(t))', color='r')
plt.xlabel('Time (s)')
plt.ylabel('Voltage (V)')
plt.title('Voltage across Inductor in Series RLC Circuit')
plt.legend()

plt.tight_layout()
plt.show()
```

Step 4: Interpret the Results

The plot generated will show the current and the voltage across the inductor as functions of time. In a real-world scenario, this simulation can help engineers understand how the circuit behaves in different conditions, such as varying resistance or capacitance, and optimize the design for specific requirements like damping, frequency response, or resonance.

Real-World Example: Simulating an AC Circuit with Python

In addition to DC circuits, AC (alternating current) circuits are widely used in electrical engineering. Python can also be used to simulate AC circuits, such as analyzing the behavior of a circuit with sinusoidal inputs.

For example, let's simulate a simple AC circuit with a resistor and an inductor in series. The voltage source is a sinusoidal function:

$V(t)=V0\sin(\omega t)V(t) = V\_0 \sin(\omega t)V(t)=V0\sin(\omega t)$

Where:

- $V0V\_0V0$ is the peak voltage.
- $\omega\backslash omega\omega$ is the angular frequency of the AC signal.

We can use the same principles as the RLC circuit simulation, but now with a sinusoidal voltage source.

python

```
# Modify the RLC system to handle AC input
def ac_rlc_circuit(t, y):
    i, v_L = y
    V_ac = V * np.sin(2 * np.pi * 50 * t)  # 50 Hz AC voltage
    di_dt = v_L
    dv_L_dt = (V_ac - R*i - (1/C)*i) / L
    return [di_dt, dv_L_dt]


# Solve the differential equations for AC circuit
solution_ac = integrate.odeint(ac_rlc_circuit, y0, t)


# Extract the current and voltage for the AC circuit
current_ac = solution_ac[:, 0]
voltage_L_ac = solution_ac[:, 1]
```

```
# Plot the results for AC circuit
plt.figure(figsize=(10, 6))
plt.subplot(2, 1, 1)
plt.plot(t, current_ac, label='Current (i(t))', color='b')
plt.xlabel('Time (s)')
plt.ylabel('Current (A)')
plt.title('Current in Series RLC AC Circuit')
plt.legend()

plt.subplot(2, 1, 2)
plt.plot(t, voltage_L_ac, label='Voltage across Inductor (v_L(t))', color='r')
plt.xlabel('Time (s)')
plt.ylabel('Voltage (V)')
plt.title('Voltage across Inductor in Series RLC AC Circuit')
plt.legend()

plt.tight_layout()
plt.show()
```

This simulation allows electrical engineers to understand the behavior of AC circuits, such as resonance, phase shift, and impedance.

Python provides electrical engineers with an accessible and flexible tool for simulating a wide variety of electrical systems, from simple circuits to more complex systems involving alternating currents and resonant behaviors. By combining Python's powerful libraries, such as NumPy, SciPy, and PySpice, engineers can quickly prototype, test, and optimize circuits for real-world applications. In this chapter, we covered the basics of simulating RLC circuits, both DC and AC, and explored how to use Python for signal analysis, optimization, and visualization of electrical systems. These skills can be applied in real-world electrical design, power systems, telecommunications, and more, making Python an essential tool for modern electrical engineers.

Chapter 15: Mechanical Engineering – Fluid Dynamics and Thermodynamics

In mechanical engineering, fluid dynamics and thermodynamics are foundational fields that involve the study of forces and energy within systems involving fluids (liquids and gases). These disciplines are essential in a variety of engineering applications, including the design of engines, HVAC systems, fluid transport, and energy generation. Python has become an invaluable tool in simulating and solving complex problems in these areas. By leveraging Python's scientific libraries, engineers can model real-world physical processes, predict system behaviors, and optimize designs without the need for expensive or complex proprietary software.

In this chapter, we will explore how Python can be used to solve problems related to fluid dynamics and thermodynamics. We'll cover key concepts and tools, providing you with real-world examples that you can apply directly to engineering problems.

1. Introduction to Fluid Dynamics and Thermodynamics Simulations

Fluid dynamics and thermodynamics are deeply interrelated areas of study. Fluid dynamics focuses on the behavior of fluids in motion, while thermodynamics deals with the flow of heat and its relationship with energy transformations. Both fields require complex mathematical models, but Python, with its easy-to-use syntax and powerful libraries, simplifies these processes.

Fluid Dynamics Simulations

Fluid dynamics involves solving the governing equations of fluid motion, which typically include the **Navier-Stokes equations** and the **Bernoulli equation**. These equations describe the behavior of fluids under various conditions, such as steady or turbulent flow, compressible or incompressible fluids, and laminar or turbulent flow regimes.

Thermodynamic Simulations

Thermodynamics, on the other hand, focuses on the study of energy transfer, heat, work, and the properties of systems at equilibrium. Python can be used to simulate heat transfer, engine performance, and more, often through solving energy balance equations, such as those found in the **First and Second Laws of Thermodynamics**.

Key Libraries for Fluid Dynamics and Thermodynamics

- **NumPy**: For numerical computations, such as solving differential equations.
- **SciPy**: For advanced numerical methods, such as solving fluid dynamics equations, and optimization problems.
- **SymPy**: For symbolic mathematics, allowing the derivation of equations and analytic solutions.

- **Matplotlib**: For visualization of fluid flow and thermodynamic processes.
- **OpenFOAM and PyFoam**: Open-source tools often interfaced with Python for computational fluid dynamics (CFD) simulations.

2. Real-World Example: Simulating Heat Transfer or Fluid Flow in Python

Example 1: Simulating Heat Transfer in a Metal Rod

Consider a simple problem in thermodynamics: determining how heat diffuses along a metal rod over time. This type of problem can be modeled using the **heat equation**, which describes the distribution of heat (temperature) in a given region over time.

The general form of the heat equation is:

$$\frac{\partial T}{\partial t} = \alpha \nabla^2 T$$

Where:

- T is the temperature.
- t is time.
- α is the thermal diffusivity.
- $\nabla^2 T$ is the Laplacian operator (second spatial derivative of temperature).

Python Solution:

Using Python, we can discretize the heat equation using the finite difference method (FDM), a common numerical technique used for solving partial differential equations. The finite difference method involves approximating derivatives with finite differences.

Here's a basic example of how to implement heat transfer in a metal rod:

python

```python
import numpy as np
import matplotlib.pyplot as plt

# Parameters
length = 10  # length of the rod in meters
time_steps = 1000  # number of time steps
n_points = 50  # number of spatial points
alpha = 0.01  # thermal diffusivity (m^2/s)
dx = length / (n_points - 1)
dt = 0.01  # time step (s)

# Initial temperature distribution (initially at 0 degrees)
T = np.zeros(n_points)

# Boundary conditions: constant temperature at both ends
T[0] = 100  # left end
T[-1] = 50  # right end

# Time loop for heat diffusion
```

```
for t in range(time_steps):
    T_new = T.copy()
    for i in range(1, n_points - 1):
        T_new[i] = T[i] + alpha * dt / dx**2 * (T[i+1] - 2*T[i] + T[i-1])
    T = T_new

    # Plot temperature distribution at each time step
    if t % 100 == 0:  # Plot every 100 time steps
        plt.plot(np.linspace(0, length, n_points), T, label=f'Time: {t*dt}s')

# Show plot
plt.xlabel('Position along the rod (m)')
plt.ylabel('Temperature (°C)')
plt.title('Heat Diffusion in a Metal Rod')
plt.legend()
plt.show()
```

Explanation:

1. **Initial Conditions**: We set the temperature at both ends of the rod and assume an initial temperature distribution of zero throughout the rod.

2. **Finite Difference Method**: For each time step, the temperature at each point is updated based on its neighbors using the heat equation.

3. **Plotting**: The temperature distribution is plotted over time to visualize how the heat diffuses through the rod.

This simulation can be extended to more complex geometries, varying materials, and dynamic boundary conditions. It's a simple but effective way of modeling heat transfer in a system.

Example 2: Simulating Fluid Flow in a Pipe

Fluid flow problems are fundamental in mechanical engineering, especially in systems like HVAC, pipelines, and fluid transport. One common model for fluid flow in pipes is the **Darcy-Weisbach equation**, which relates the pressure drop in a pipe to the flow rate, pipe dimensions, and friction factor.

The Darcy-Weisbach equation is:

$$\Delta P = f \cdot \frac{L}{D} \cdot \frac{\rho v^2}{2}$$

Where:

- ΔP is the pressure drop (Pa).
- f is the Darcy friction factor.
- L is the length of the pipe (m).
- D is the diameter of the pipe (m).
- ρ is the density of the fluid (kg/m³).
- v is the velocity of the fluid (m/s).

Python Solution:

We can use Python to compute the pressure drop in a pipe based on the given parameters.

python

```
# Parameters for pipe flow
length = 100  # pipe length in meters
diameter = 0.1  # pipe diameter in meters
density = 1000  # density of water in kg/m^3
velocity = 1.5  # velocity of fluid in m/s
friction_factor = 0.02  # Darcy friction factor (for turbulent flow)

# Calculate pressure drop using the Darcy-Weisbach equation
pressure_drop = friction_factor * (length / diameter) * (density * velocity**2) /
2
print(f"Pressure drop: {pressure_drop:.2f} Pa")
```

This program calculates the pressure drop in a water pipe, which is essential for designing and optimizing fluid systems.

3.

Python is a versatile tool for solving problems in fluid dynamics and thermodynamics. Its rich ecosystem of libraries, such as **SciPy**, **NumPy**, and **SymPy**, makes it easy to model complex physical systems and simulate real-world engineering scenarios. Whether you're simulating heat transfer in solids or fluid flow through pipes, Python provides a powerful platform for solving engineering problems and gaining valuable insights. The examples in this chapter demonstrate the simplicity and effectiveness of Python in tackling fundamental mechanical engineering challenges.

By mastering these techniques, engineers can harness Python to solve a broad range of problems in fluid dynamics and thermodynamics, optimizing designs and improving system performance.

Chapter 16: Robotics Programming in Python

Robotics is a dynamic and interdisciplinary field that combines elements of mechanical engineering, electrical engineering, and computer science. With the advent of accessible computing power and sophisticated software tools, robotics has become a critical component in manufacturing, healthcare, space exploration, and various other industries. In this context, Python has emerged as a popular programming language for developing robotic applications, due to its simplicity, flexibility, and the extensive ecosystem of libraries and frameworks available for hardware interfacing, control, and simulation.

This chapter will guide you through the basics of robotics programming using Python, demonstrating how Python can be employed to control robotic systems and automate tasks. We'll explore the key concepts of robotics, how Python interfaces with hardware, and how to use Python to control robotic movements and behavior.

1. Introduction to Robotics

Robotics refers to the design, construction, operation, and use of robots, which are programmable machines capable of performing tasks autonomously or semi-autonomously. The core components of a robot typically include sensors (for feedback), actuators (for movement), and a control system that processes inputs and commands actions.

Python's role in robotics is multifaceted. It can be used for simulation, control, and communication with embedded systems that govern the robot's hardware. Many robots, including robotic arms, drones, and mobile robots, can be controlled by Python scripts, making it a popular choice for both amateur and professional roboticists.

Some of the key areas where Python is applied in robotics include:

- **Motion Control**: Programming the movement of robotic arms, legs, or wheels.
- **Sensor Integration**: Reading and processing sensor data to control the robot's actions based on environmental feedback.
- **Path Planning**: Programming robots to navigate through environments while avoiding obstacles.
- **Machine Vision**: Enabling robots to "see" the environment using cameras and sensors, then process the visual data to make decisions.

Python libraries such as RPi.GPIO for Raspberry Pi, pySerial for serial communication, and pyRobot for controlling robotic arms provide easy-to-use interfaces for controlling hardware. Additionally, frameworks like ROS (Robot Operating System) support Python, enabling complex tasks such as pathfinding and object recognition.

2. Working with Robotic Arms Using Python

One of the most common robotics applications is the control of robotic arms, which are used in industries like manufacturing, assembly, and packaging. These robotic arms can perform a wide range of tasks, from precise pick-and-place operations to complex assembly procedures. Controlling the movement of a robotic arm requires programming its joints and actuators to follow a specific set of instructions.

In Python, robotic arm control typically involves the following key components:

- **Inverse Kinematics**: This refers to the mathematical process of calculating the necessary joint angles that will position the end effector (the hand or tool of the robotic arm) at a desired location in space.
- **Motion Planning**: Programming the arm to follow a path that avoids obstacles and reaches the target location in a controlled manner.
- **Sensor Feedback**: Robots often rely on feedback from sensors (e.g., force sensors, position sensors) to adjust their movements and interact with objects in their environment.

Key Libraries for Robotic Control

- **pySerial**: A Python library for serial communication that allows Python scripts to send and receive data from microcontrollers and embedded devices.
- **RPi.GPIO**: A library that interfaces with the GPIO pins of the Raspberry Pi, allowing for control of motors and other hardware.
- **pyRobot**: A high-level robotics framework designed to work with various robotic platforms, allowing easy control of robotic arms.
- **ROS (Robot Operating System)**: A flexible framework for building robotic systems, ROS supports Python for developing control nodes, interfacing with hardware, and handling communication between different parts of a robotic system.

Controlling a Robotic Arm

Let's walk through an example of controlling a robotic arm using Python. In this case, we'll simulate controlling a robotic arm with a 3-joint configuration, where each joint is powered by a motor.

Step-by-Step Example: Controlling a Robotic Arm

1. **Hardware Setup**:
   o A robotic arm with motors controlled by an embedded system (such as Arduino, Raspberry Pi, or a dedicated controller).

- o Sensors (optional) to provide feedback on joint angles and end effector position.

2. **Libraries**: Install the required libraries using pip:

bash

pip install pySerial

3. **Writing Python Code**: We will write a Python script to move the arm's joints. In this simplified example, we'll use a motor control library that interfaces with an Arduino.

python

```python
import serial
import time

# Open the serial connection to Arduino (Replace with your port)
arduino = serial.Serial('COM3', 9600)

# Function to move the robotic arm
def move_arm(joint1_angle, joint2_angle, joint3_angle):
    # Send joint angles to Arduino via serial communication
    command = f"{joint1_angle},{joint2_angle},{joint3_angle}\n"
    arduino.write(command.encode())

# Move the arm to a specific position
move_arm(45, 90, 120)

# Wait for a moment to see the result
```

time.sleep(2)

# Move the arm to another position
move_arm(90, 180, 30)

# Close the serial connection
arduino.close()

In this code:

- We use the pySerial library to communicate with the Arduino.
- The move_arm() function sends the desired angles for each joint to the robotic arm.
- The values are sent as a comma-separated string, which the Arduino interprets to adjust the motor positions.

4. **Arduino Code**: The Arduino code listens for serial input and adjusts the motors accordingly:

cpp

```cpp
#include <Servo.h>

Servo joint1, joint2, joint3;

void setup() {
  joint1.attach(9); // Attach motors to pins
  joint2.attach(10);
  joint3.attach(11);
```

```
Serial.begin(9600);
}

void loop() {
 if (Serial.available() > 0) {
   String data = Serial.readStringUntil('\n');
   int joint1_angle = data.substring(0, data.indexOf(',')).toInt();
   int        joint2_angle        =        data.substring(data.indexOf(',')+1,
data.lastIndexOf(',')).toInt();
   int joint3_angle = data.substring(data.lastIndexOf(',')+1).toInt();

   joint1.write(joint1_angle);
   joint2.write(joint2_angle);
   joint3.write(joint3_angle);
 }
}
```

This Arduino code reads the serial input from Python, splits the data, and adjusts the positions of the robotic arm's joints.

3. Real-World Applications in Robotics

Robotic programming in Python has wide applications across multiple industries. Here are some of the notable use cases:

- **Manufacturing Automation**: Robots in production lines that handle assembly, packing, or sorting. Python can control the robots, integrating them with factory systems.
- **Medical Robotics**: Python is used to control robotic surgical tools, assistive devices, and rehabilitation robots. Precision control and sensor feedback are key here.

- **Robotic Exploration**: Python is used in autonomous robots for exploring planets or hazardous environments. It's often employed in robot simulation, control, and planning tasks.
- **Education and Research**: Many robotic platforms, such as Arduino or Raspberry Pi, support Python for controlling robots, making it a favorite among educators and researchers.

4.

In this chapter, we've explored the role of Python in robotics, from controlling robotic arms to building real-world applications. By using Python's rich set of libraries and frameworks, engineers can model, simulate, and control robotic systems efficiently. As robotics continues to evolve, Python's simplicity and power will make it an essential tool for developing cutting-edge robotic technologies.

In the next chapter, we will dive deeper into advanced control techniques and real-time programming, essential for robotics applications requiring high-performance control and low-latency responses.

Chapter 17: Python for Civil Engineering – Surveying and Site Analysis

Civil engineering is a broad discipline that deals with the design, construction, and maintenance of infrastructure, such as bridges, roads, buildings, and water supply systems. It involves a deep understanding of environmental conditions, site-specific challenges, and structural requirements. One of the critical tasks in civil engineering is surveying and site analysis, which involves collecting, processing, and analyzing geographic and environmental data to inform design and construction decisions.

With the growing reliance on data-driven decision-making, Python has emerged as a powerful tool in civil engineering for automating tasks, performing complex calculations, and visualizing data. Python's ability to handle geographical and spatial data makes it an ideal language for surveying, site analysis, and terrain modeling.

In this chapter, we will explore how Python can be used in civil engineering to support surveying and site analysis tasks. From processing elevation data to analyzing geographic coordinates, Python allows civil engineers to work efficiently with large datasets and produce accurate models for construction projects.

1. Using Python in Civil Engineering

Civil engineers often work with complex datasets that contain geographical, environmental, and structural information. Python's rich ecosystem of libraries, such as NumPy, Pandas, Matplotlib, Geopandas, and Shapely, can be used to perform data manipulation, mathematical calculations, and spatial analysis. Python enables engineers to:

- **Process Geographical Data**: Python can read, clean, and transform large geographic datasets, such as GPS coordinates, elevation maps, and survey data.
- **Perform Geospatial Analysis**: Python libraries such as Geopandas allow engineers to conduct spatial analysis and determine factors like terrain elevation, distances between landmarks, and the suitability of locations for construction.
- **Create Visualizations**: Python's visualization libraries, such as Matplotlib and Plotly, can be used to generate 2D and 3D visualizations of sites, helping engineers understand terrain features and design implications.
- **Automate Repetitive Tasks**: Python can automate tasks like data cleaning, file processing, and batch calculations, saving time and reducing the risk of human error.

Python also integrates well with Geographic Information Systems (GIS), allowing engineers to interact with GIS data formats like GeoJSON and shapefiles. By using Python to automate GIS workflows, civil engineers can focus more on problem-solving and less on manual data entry.

2. Surveying Tools and Site Analysis Through Python

Surveying is one of the first steps in any civil engineering project, and it involves collecting data related to the land, topography, and environmental features of a site. Python provides a versatile platform for automating many aspects of surveying, including data collection, analysis, and visualization.

Geospatial Data Processing

Surveying often involves handling large datasets that contain latitude and longitude coordinates, elevation values, and other geospatial information. Python's libraries can be used to process this data and convert it into usable formats for analysis.

For example, Python can be used to process GPS coordinates, convert them into a Cartesian coordinate system, and calculate distances, areas, and angles. By using the Geopandas library, Python can read and manipulate geospatial data, allowing engineers to visualize and analyze the terrain.

Site Analysis Using Elevation and Terrain Data

One of the key aspects of site analysis is assessing the terrain's elevation, slope, and suitability for construction. Python can be used to analyze Digital Elevation Models (DEMs), which represent the Earth's surface in terms of elevation. These models are often used in civil engineering projects to evaluate the feasibility of construction in a specific area.

Python, in combination with Pandas and NumPy, can be used to analyze terrain elevation data to calculate the slope of the land, determine areas prone to flooding, or assess the potential for soil erosion. This is particularly useful in large-scale construction projects, where a comprehensive understanding of the terrain is crucial.

3. *Real-World Example – Processing Geographical and Elevation Data for Construction Planning*

To demonstrate how Python can be applied in civil engineering for surveying and site analysis, let's walk through a real-world example of how Python can be used to process geographical and elevation data for construction planning.

Scenario:

A construction company is planning to build a new road through a rural area. The first step is to analyze the land's topography and assess its suitability for construction. The engineers need to process elevation data to determine the slope of the land and identify any potential challenges, such as steep gradients, areas prone to flooding, or potential hazards related to terrain instability.

Step 1: Loading and Processing the Elevation Data

The elevation data is stored in a GeoTIFF file, a common format for raster data. Python's rasterio library can be used to load the data and convert it into a NumPy array for further analysis.

python

```
import rasterio
import numpy as np

# Load the elevation data (GeoTIFF file)
with rasterio.open('elevation_data.tif') as dataset:
    elevation_data = dataset.read(1)  # Read the first band (elevation)

# Print basic statistics about the elevation data
print("Min Elevation:", np.min(elevation_data))
print("Max Elevation:", np.max(elevation_data))
```

Step 2: Analyzing the Slope

Using the elevation data, we can calculate the slope of the terrain, which is crucial for road planning. The slope can be calculated by determining the change in elevation between neighboring cells.

python

```
from scipy import gradient

# Calculate the gradient (slope) of the elevation data
slope_x, slope_y = gradient(elevation_data)
slope = np.sqrt(slope_x**2 + slope_y**2)
```

```
# Visualize the slope
import matplotlib.pyplot as plt
plt.imshow(slope, cmap='viridis')
plt.colorbar(label='Slope (degrees)')
plt.title('Terrain Slope')
plt.show()
```

Step 3: Identifying Flood-Prone Areas

Flood-prone areas can be identified by comparing the elevation data to a threshold value. For example, areas with an elevation below a certain level may be at risk of flooding.

python

```
# Define a threshold for flood-prone areas (elevation below 50 meters)
flood_threshold = 50
flood_prone_areas = elevation_data < flood_threshold

# Visualize flood-prone areas
plt.imshow(flood_prone_areas, cmap='coolwarm')
plt.colorbar(label='Flood-prone Areas')
plt.title('Flood Risk Areas')
plt.show()
```

Step 4:

By processing and analyzing the elevation data, Python enables civil engineers to visualize and identify key features of the terrain, such as slopes and flood-prone areas. This information is essential for making informed decisions about road construction and helps ensure that the project is completed safely and efficiently.

4.

Python has become an indispensable tool for civil engineers working in surveying, site analysis, and construction planning. With its ability to process geographical data, perform mathematical calculations, and create visualizations, Python empowers engineers to analyze complex site conditions, model terrain features, and make data-driven decisions for their projects. By leveraging Python's robust libraries, engineers can significantly improve the accuracy, efficiency, and effectiveness of their work, ensuring that infrastructure projects are designed and executed with precision.

In this chapter, we covered the use of Python in processing geographical and elevation data, performing site analysis, and modeling terrain features for construction planning. Through real-world examples and practical applications, we demonstrated how Python can be used to address common challenges in civil engineering, ultimately leading to better, more informed decision-making.

Chapter 18: Machine Learning for Engineering

In recent years, the integration of machine learning (ML) into engineering has revolutionized many fields, offering powerful tools for prediction, optimization, and decision-making. Traditionally, engineers relied on mathematical models, simulations, and expert knowledge to solve complex problems. However, with the advent of machine learning, engineers now have the capability to analyze large volumes of data, uncover hidden patterns, and predict outcomes with remarkable accuracy.

Machine learning offers a way to automate decision-making and provide valuable insights that were previously difficult or impossible to obtain using traditional engineering methods. Whether it is predicting the failure of mechanical components, optimizing manufacturing processes, or improving system efficiency, machine learning models are being used to improve designs and drive innovations across industries.

In this chapter, we will explore how Python and machine learning can be applied in engineering. We will start by discussing the basics of machine learning, its types, and how it can be used to solve engineering problems. Then, we will dive into key Python libraries used for machine learning, such as Scikit-learn,

TensorFlow, and Keras, and show how they can be used to build predictive models for engineering applications.

1. Introduction to Machine Learning in Engineering

Machine learning, a subfield of artificial intelligence (AI), focuses on developing algorithms that allow computers to learn from and make decisions based on data. Unlike traditional programming, where specific rules are written by humans to solve a problem, machine learning enables systems to learn from experience and improve over time without explicit programming.

In engineering, machine learning can be applied to various tasks such as:

- **Predictive Maintenance:** Using historical data to predict the failure of components or systems before they break down, enabling proactive maintenance and reducing downtime.
- **Optimization:** Applying ML algorithms to optimize designs, manufacturing processes, or operations to minimize costs, improve efficiency, and enhance performance.
- **Quality Control:** Identifying patterns in production data to detect anomalies or defects in real-time and improving quality assurance processes.
- **System Simulation and Modeling:** Leveraging ML to simulate complex systems and predict behaviors under

different conditions, helping to reduce the time and cost of physical prototypes and tests.

2. Key Machine Learning Libraries for Engineering

Python offers a rich ecosystem of libraries that are extensively used in machine learning for engineering tasks. Here, we will cover three of the most popular libraries: Scikit-learn, TensorFlow, and Keras.

Scikit-learn: Scikit-learn is one of the most widely used Python libraries for machine learning. It provides simple and efficient tools for data analysis and modeling, with a focus on ease of use and flexibility. It includes various machine learning algorithms for classification, regression, clustering, and dimensionality reduction, among others. Scikit-learn is highly suitable for small to medium-sized datasets and is a great starting point for engineers new to machine learning.

TensorFlow: TensorFlow is an open-source library developed by Google for building and deploying machine learning models, particularly deep learning models. While Scikit-learn is great for traditional ML algorithms, TensorFlow is specifically designed for deep learning, which requires handling large datasets and building complex neural networks. Engineers working with image recognition, speech processing, and other deep learning applications often use TensorFlow.

Keras: Keras is a high-level neural networks API that runs on top of TensorFlow. It allows for rapid prototyping and experimentation with deep learning models. Keras is user-friendly and simplifies the process of building and training deep learning models, making it a great choice for engineers who want to leverage neural networks without diving into the complexities of TensorFlow.

3. Real-World Example: Predicting Mechanical Component Failure Using Machine Learning

In engineering, particularly in fields such as mechanical engineering, one of the most critical tasks is ensuring the reliability and safety of components. Predicting the failure of mechanical components, such as bearings, gears, or turbines, is essential for preventing costly downtime, improving safety, and reducing maintenance costs.

Step 1: Collecting Data The first step in building a machine learning model for predicting component failure is to collect relevant data. In this case, data might include:

- Sensor data (vibration, temperature, pressure)
- Historical maintenance records
- Usage patterns (e.g., load, speed, operating conditions)
- Failure logs (types of failure, timestamps, etc.)

This data can come from multiple sources such as sensors on machinery, logs from monitoring systems, and past maintenance records.

Step 2: Preprocessing Data Once the data is collected, the next step is preprocessing it for use in a machine learning model. This can involve:

- **Cleaning**: Handling missing values, outliers, and noisy data.
- **Normalization/Standardization**: Scaling numerical data so that it fits within a specific range or has a mean of zero and standard deviation of one.
- **Feature Engineering**: Creating new features from raw data (e.g., extracting trends or calculating moving averages).
- **Splitting Data**: Dividing the dataset into training, validation, and testing sets.

Step 3: Selecting and Training the Model In this step, engineers can choose the appropriate machine learning algorithm based on the data and the problem at hand. Common algorithms for predictive maintenance include:

- **Classification algorithms** (e.g., Logistic Regression, Random Forest, Support Vector Machines) for predicting whether a component will fail or not.

- **Regression algorithms** (e.g., Linear Regression, Decision Trees) for predicting the remaining useful life (RUL) of the component.

The chosen algorithm is then trained using the training dataset, which means adjusting the model's parameters to minimize the error in predictions.

Step 4: Evaluating the Model Once the model is trained, it is evaluated on the test dataset to measure its performance. Common evaluation metrics for predictive models include:

- **Accuracy**: The percentage of correct predictions.
- **Precision and Recall**: Measures for classification problems to evaluate how well the model identifies positive instances.
- **Root Mean Squared Error (RMSE)**: For regression tasks, this metric measures the difference between predicted and actual values.

Step 5: Deploying the Model Once the model has been trained and evaluated, it can be deployed in a real-time environment. For example, sensors attached to the machinery can continuously send data to a system where the trained model predicts the likelihood of failure. Based on these predictions, maintenance actions can be taken proactively.

4. Real-World Example: Using Scikit-learn to Build a Predictive Maintenance Model

In this example, we will use Python's Scikit-learn library to create a basic predictive maintenance model based on sensor data. We will demonstrate the steps of collecting data, preprocessing it, and training a classification model to predict whether a mechanical component will fail within a given time frame.

python

```python
import pandas as pd
from sklearn.model_selection import train_test_split
from sklearn.ensemble import RandomForestClassifier
from sklearn.metrics import classification_report, accuracy_score

# Load data (example: sensor data and failure labels)
data = pd.read_csv('sensor_data.csv')

# Preprocessing: Handle missing values, encode categorical data, etc.
data.fillna(method='ffill', inplace=True)

# Features and labels
X = data.drop('failure', axis=1)  # Features
y = data['failure']  # Labels (1: failure, 0: no failure)

# Train-test split
X_train, X_test, y_train, y_test = train_test_split(X, y, test_size=0.3, random_state=42)
```

```
# Build and train a Random Forest classifier
clf = RandomForestClassifier(n_estimators=100, random_state=42)
clf.fit(X_train, y_train)

# Predictions
y_pred = clf.predict(X_test)

# Evaluate model
print(f"Accuracy: {accuracy_score(y_test, y_pred)}")
print(f"Classification Report:\n{classification_report(y_test, y_pred)}")
```

In this code, we use a Random Forest classifier to predict whether a mechanical component will fail based on the sensor data. We evaluate the model using accuracy and classification report metrics.

5.

Machine learning is an invaluable tool for engineers looking to predict, optimize, and improve their processes. By leveraging Python and libraries like Scikit-learn, TensorFlow, and Keras, engineers can build predictive models that enhance efficiency, improve safety, and reduce costs. Whether it is predicting equipment failure, optimizing material usage, or improving design, machine learning provides engineers with powerful methods to tackle complex problems and make data-driven decisions.

Chapter 19: Data Science for Engineering – Data Collection, Cleaning, and Analysis

In the age of digital transformation, engineering is increasingly driven by data. Engineers now have access to a wealth of information from sensors, monitoring systems, production logs, and simulations, which can provide valuable insights into system performance, maintenance needs, and design optimizations. However, to make the most of this data, it needs to be properly collected, cleaned, and analyzed.

Data science provides a structured approach to processing, analyzing, and interpreting complex datasets, making it an essential skill for engineers. The ability to clean and process raw data, analyze trends, and derive actionable insights from large volumes of information is a critical capability in fields such as mechanical engineering, civil engineering, electrical engineering, and more.

In this chapter, we will focus on how Python can be used to handle engineering datasets and perform data science tasks such as data collection, cleaning, and analysis. By leveraging libraries such as Pandas, NumPy, and Matplotlib, engineers can turn messy, unstructured data into valuable information that helps optimize designs and systems.

We will begin by discussing the various stages of the data science process in the context of engineering. Then, we will explore the tools and techniques used for data collection and cleaning. Finally, we will walk through a real-world example of analyzing sensor data collected from an industrial system, and show how Python can help in extracting useful insights for improving system performance.

Introduction to Data Science in Engineering

Data science in engineering refers to the use of advanced analytics techniques to derive insights from engineering data. Engineers generate vast amounts of data during experiments, simulations, and real-time system monitoring. These datasets often contain valuable information that can be leveraged to improve designs, optimize processes, and predict future outcomes.

The process of data science in engineering typically involves the following stages:

1. **Data Collection**: Gathering data from various sources such as sensors, machines, databases, or simulations.
2. **Data Cleaning**: Removing or correcting invalid, incomplete, or inconsistent data.

3. **Data Analysis**: Applying statistical and computational methods to explore the data and uncover patterns.

4. **Data Visualization**: Presenting data in graphical formats to make trends and insights more accessible.

5. **Predictive Analytics**: Using machine learning models to predict future behavior or outcomes based on historical data.

Python is an ideal tool for engineers due to its wide range of libraries and ease of use for handling large datasets. It simplifies the process of data collection, cleaning, analysis, and visualization. Engineers can take advantage of Python's powerful capabilities to make data-driven decisions and automate tasks.

Key Libraries for Data Science in Engineering

Before diving into the practical aspects of data science in engineering, let's briefly explore the key Python libraries that facilitate the process:

1. **Pandas**: Pandas is the go-to library for handling structured data (i.e., data in tables). It provides DataFrame and Series objects, which allow engineers to manipulate, filter, and analyze data efficiently. Pandas is indispensable for tasks such as data cleaning, grouping, aggregation, and pivoting.

2. **NumPy**: NumPy provides support for large, multi-dimensional arrays and matrices, and it comes with a wide range of mathematical functions. It is ideal for numerical data processing and performing mathematical operations on datasets.

3. **Matplotlib and Seaborn**: These are the primary libraries for data visualization in Python. Matplotlib allows for the creation of static, interactive, and animated plots, while Seaborn builds on Matplotlib to simplify the creation of complex visualizations such as heatmaps, pairplots, and statistical graphics.

4. **SciPy**: SciPy extends NumPy and provides a large collection of numerical algorithms for optimization, integration, interpolation, eigenvalue problems, and other engineering computations.

5. **Scikit-learn**: Scikit-learn is a powerful library for machine learning that allows engineers to implement models for regression, classification, clustering, and dimensionality reduction. It's especially useful for predictive analytics in engineering.

Real-World Example: Cleaning and Analyzing Sensor Data

In this section, we will walk through an example of how Python can be used to clean and analyze sensor data from an industrial system. For simplicity, let's assume that we are working with data collected from temperature sensors monitoring the performance of a machine. This type of data can be noisy, incomplete, or contain outliers, and our goal is to clean the data, analyze it for trends, and visualize the results.

Step 1: Data Collection

Typically, data is collected from sensors and stored in a CSV file or database. In this example, let's assume we have a CSV file containing temperature readings over time.

Example of a sample data file:

Timestamp	Sensor ID	Temperature (°C)
2024-01-01 00:00:00	101	45.5
2024-01-01 00:01:00	101	46.1
2024-01-01 00:02:00	101	45.8
2024-01-01 00:03:00	101	0.0
2024-01-01 00:04:00	101	46.3
...	...	...

The data file might contain incorrect readings, such as the temperature reading of 0°C, which is clearly an outlier or an invalid entry.

Step 2: Data Cleaning

Python's Pandas library can be used to load the CSV file and perform cleaning operations. For example, we can remove or impute missing values, correct invalid data, and filter out outliers.

python

```python
import pandas as pd

# Load the sensor data
data = pd.read_csv('sensor_data.csv')

# Remove rows with invalid readings (e.g., temperature 0.0°C)
data = data[data['Temperature (°C)'] > 0]

# Fill missing values with the mean temperature
data['Temperature (°C)'].fillna(data['Temperature (°C)'].mean(), inplace=True)

# Print the cleaned data
print(data.head())
```

Step 3: Data Analysis

Once the data is cleaned, we can perform exploratory data analysis (EDA) to identify patterns or trends. We can calculate basic statistics such as the mean, median, standard deviation, and visualize the distribution of temperatures.

python

```python
# Basic statistical analysis
mean_temp = data['Temperature (°C)'].mean()
std_temp = data['Temperature (°C)'].std()

# Display statistics
print(f'Mean Temperature: {mean_temp}°C')
print(f'Standard Deviation: {std_temp}°C')

# Visualizing the data
import matplotlib.pyplot as plt

plt.plot(data['Timestamp'], data['Temperature (°C)'])
plt.title('Temperature Readings Over Time')
plt.xlabel('Time')
plt.ylabel('Temperature (°C)')
plt.xticks(rotation=45)
plt.show()
```

Step 4: Data Interpretation

After analyzing the data, engineers can interpret the results. For instance, if the temperature of a machine is gradually increasing over time, this might indicate an issue with the cooling system, which could warrant a maintenance check.

In this chapter, we've explored how data science is applied to engineering problems, focusing on data collection, cleaning, and analysis. Using Python's powerful libraries, engineers can process and analyze vast amounts of data, uncover meaningful patterns, and make data-driven decisions to improve system performance.

Through the real-world example of analyzing sensor data, we've seen how Python can simplify the data science workflow, making it accessible and practical for engineers. The ability to clean and analyze data efficiently allows engineers to focus on solving complex problems, optimizing processes, and driving innovation in their respective fields.

Chapter 20: Python for Environmental Engineering

Environmental engineering involves the application of scientific principles to protect and improve the environment, making it a crucial field for sustainable development. From modeling pollutant dispersion to designing water treatment systems, environmental engineers face complex challenges that require effective tools for data analysis, modeling, and simulation.

Python has become an indispensable tool for environmental engineers due to its versatility, ease of use, and the vast ecosystem of libraries that enable data analysis, simulation, and visualization. In this chapter, we will explore how Python can be leveraged to model environmental systems, handle environmental data, and simulate real-world scenarios related to pollution, water quality, climate, and more.

Environmental Data and Modeling

Environmental systems are highly complex, consisting of multiple variables and factors that interact in nonlinear ways. To make informed decisions, environmental engineers rely on accurate models that can simulate the behavior of various components in these systems—such as the dispersion of pollutants in the air, water, or soil.

1. Modeling Environmental Systems

Python's powerful libraries, like NumPy and SciPy, allow environmental engineers to create numerical models that simulate real-world phenomena. Whether it's modeling the movement of water through soil in hydrology, simulating air quality in urban environments, or predicting the effects of climate change, Python can handle the heavy computational needs of these tasks. Libraries like SymPy (for symbolic mathematics) and PySCeS (for chemical and biochemical system simulation) are also commonly used in this domain.

- **Pollutant Dispersion**: In environmental engineering, understanding how pollutants disperse in the atmosphere or water bodies is critical for assessing the impact on human health and ecosystems. Mathematical models like Gaussian Plume and Lagrangian models are commonly used to predict the distribution of airborne pollutants. Python's ability to solve partial differential equations (PDEs) makes it an excellent tool for this type of modeling.

2. Data Collection and Preprocessing

Environmental data is often collected via sensors or satellite imagery and stored in formats like CSV, JSON, or databases. Using Python's powerful libraries, engineers can efficiently import, clean, and preprocess large datasets. Pandas is commonly used to handle tabular data, allowing engineers to remove duplicates, handle missing values, and manipulate the data into a usable format for further analysis.

- **Example**: Handling air quality data from various sensors in a city's monitoring system. Python can be used to clean and preprocess this data, ensuring that it is accurate and ready for further analysis.

3. Data Analysis and Visualization

Once environmental data is collected and cleaned, Python can be used to perform exploratory data analysis (EDA). With tools like Matplotlib, Seaborn, and Plotly, engineers can visualize environmental data trends, correlations, and anomalies.

- **Example**: Visualizing pollutant concentration over time or geographical locations to understand air quality patterns or trends in water pollution levels.

Real-World Example: Modeling Pollutant Dispersion in an Environment

In this section, we'll walk through an example of using Python to model pollutant dispersion in an environment, focusing on air pollution as an example. We'll create a simplified model of pollutant dispersion using the **Gaussian Plume Model**, which is widely used to estimate how pollutants spread in the atmosphere from a point source (like a factory chimney).

Step 1: Defining the Parameters

The Gaussian Plume Model is based on several parameters, such as the wind speed, atmospheric stability, and the emission rate of the pollutant. In Python, we can define these parameters as variables.

python

```python
import numpy as np
import matplotlib.pyplot as plt

# Define parameters for the Gaussian plume model
Q = 500  # Emission rate in grams per second
u = 5    # Wind speed in meters per second
H = 10   # Stack height in meters
sigma_y = 15 # Standard deviation in the y direction (crosswind) in meters
sigma_z = 10 # Standard deviation in the z direction (vertical) in meters
```

Step 2: Calculate Pollutant Concentration

The concentration of pollutants at a given point downwind from the source can be calculated using the Gaussian plume equation:

$$C(x,y,z) = \frac{Q}{2\pi u \sigma_y \sigma_z} \exp\left(-\frac{y^2}{2\sigma_y^2} \right) \exp\left(-\frac{(z-H)^2}{2\sigma_z^2} \right)$$

Where:

- $C(x,y,z)C(x,\ y,\ z)C(x,y,z)$ is the concentration of the pollutant at location $(x,y,z)(x,\ y,\ z)(x,y,z)$,
- QQQ is the emission rate,
- uuu is the wind speed,
- $\sigma y\backslash sigma\_y\sigma y$ and $\sigma z\backslash sigma\_z\sigma z$ are the dispersion coefficients,
- HHH is the height of the emission source.

python

```
def gaussian_plume(x, y, Q, u, sigma_y, sigma_z, H):
    # Calculate concentration using the Gaussian plume model
    return (Q / (2 * np.pi * u * sigma_y * sigma_z)) * np.exp(-y**2 / (2 * sigma_y**2)) * np.exp(-(z - H)**2 / (2 * sigma_z**2))

# Generate a grid of points for analysis
x = np.linspace(0, 1000, 100)  # Distance downwind
y = np.linspace(-100, 100, 200)  # Crosswind distance
X, Y = np.meshgrid(x, y)

# Calculate pollutant concentration at each point
Z = gaussian_plume(X, Y, Q, u, sigma_y, sigma_z, H)
```

Step 3: Visualization of the Pollutant Dispersion

Once we have the pollutant concentration data, we can visualize the dispersion pattern using **Matplotlib**. We can create a contour plot to show how pollutant concentration changes with distance from the source.

python

```
plt.figure(figsize=(10, 6))
cp = plt.contourf(X, Y, Z, levels=50, cmap='jet')
plt.colorbar(cp, label='Concentration (g/m³)')
plt.title('Pollutant Dispersion - Gaussian Plume Model')
plt.xlabel('Distance (m)')
plt.ylabel('Crosswind Distance (m)')
plt.show()
```

Step 4: Interpretation of Results

The contour plot generated by the model will help engineers understand how the pollutant concentration decreases with distance from the source and how atmospheric conditions (e.g., wind speed and direction) affect the dispersion.

- **Scenario**: If an engineer is studying the impact of a factory's emissions on nearby communities, this model can help predict pollutant concentrations at various distances, aiding in risk assessments and regulatory compliance.

Python provides engineers with a powerful toolkit for modeling environmental systems, simulating pollutant dispersion, and analyzing environmental data. By leveraging libraries like **NumPy**, **SciPy**, and **Matplotlib**, engineers can perform complex environmental simulations and make data-driven decisions for sustainability, pollution control, and resource management.

In this chapter, we demonstrated the application of Python in environmental engineering by modeling pollutant dispersion in the atmosphere. By utilizing Python's computational power and visualization capabilities, engineers can simulate real-world scenarios, analyze large datasets, and optimize environmental processes.

This chapter sets the stage for more advanced applications of Python in environmental monitoring, climate modeling, and sustainability efforts.

Chapter 21: Computational Fluid Dynamics (CFD) with Python

Computational Fluid Dynamics (CFD) is an essential tool in engineering for simulating and analyzing the flow of fluids—whether it's air, water, or other substances. It is used across various fields such as aerospace, mechanical, civil, and environmental engineering, providing insights into fluid behavior under different conditions. CFD simulations enable engineers to optimize designs, reduce costs, and improve performance without relying solely on physical prototypes.

Python has emerged as a powerful programming language for CFD applications due to its extensive support for numerical computations, ease of integration with other engineering tools, and availability of dedicated libraries. In this chapter, we will explore how Python can be used for CFD simulations, covering both basic and advanced techniques, and demonstrate its use in real-world engineering applications.

Introduction to Computational Fluid Dynamics (CFD)

Computational Fluid Dynamics is the branch of fluid mechanics that uses numerical methods and algorithms to analyze and solve problems related to fluid flow. CFD involves discretizing fluid domains and solving the governing equations of fluid flow—most commonly, the Navier-Stokes equations—using numerical methods.

1. Solving CFD Problems with Python

CFD simulations typically involve the following steps:

- **Defining the Problem Domain**: Setting up the geometry of the system, such as an aircraft wing, pipe, or ventilation system.
- **Meshing**: Breaking the domain into smaller elements (grid points) to solve the equations at discrete locations.
- **Solving the Governing Equations**: The equations of fluid motion, like the Navier-Stokes equations, are solved numerically at each grid point.
- **Post-Processing**: Visualizing the results to interpret the behavior of the fluid and make engineering decisions.

Python can handle all these steps with its flexibility in numerical computation, data manipulation, and visualization.

CFD Tools and Libraries in Python

Python has a number of libraries and frameworks designed specifically for CFD applications. These libraries either offer direct solutions to CFD problems or can be integrated with established CFD tools for Python-based workflows.

2. OpenFOAM and PyFoam

OpenFOAM is one of the most widely used open-source software tools for CFD simulations. It offers a comprehensive set of solvers and pre/post-processing utilities, enabling users to perform complex fluid flow analysis across a variety of industries.

PyFoam is a Python library that serves as a wrapper for OpenFOAM, enabling Python scripts to automate simulations, post-process results, and manipulate OpenFOAM data. PyFoam allows for integration with other Python-based libraries, such as NumPy for numerical operations and Matplotlib for plotting and visualizing results.

Python can also interact with OpenFOAM directly through system calls, facilitating automation, batch processing, and more flexible workflows.

3. Simulating Flow Around an Aircraft Wing

A common CFD problem in aerospace engineering is simulating the airflow over an aircraft wing to analyze its aerodynamic properties. Using Python for CFD in this scenario involves creating a simulation that models the wing geometry, the surrounding air, and the flow characteristics (e.g., velocity, pressure, and temperature).

This example demonstrates how Python can be used to:

- Create the geometry of the aircraft wing.
- Define the mesh grid for the simulation.

- Set boundary conditions, such as airflow velocity and pressure at the inlet and outlet.
- Solve the flow equations using OpenFOAM.
- Post-process and visualize the results, such as pressure distribution, drag forces, and turbulence patterns.

4. Example Code for Setting Up a CFD Simulation

Here's an example of how you might approach simulating airflow around an aircraft wing using Python:

python

```python
import numpy as np
import matplotlib.pyplot as plt
from pyfoam import OpenFOAMCase

# Define the domain and mesh
mesh      =      OpenFOAMCase.create_mesh(geometry="aircraft_wing.stl",
mesh_size=100)

# Set the boundary conditions
boundary_conditions = {
    "inlet": {"velocity": 30},  # Inlet velocity in m/s
    "outlet": {"pressure": 0},  # Outlet pressure in Pa
    "walls": {"no-slip": True},  # No-slip condition at the walls
}

# Set up solver parameters
solver = OpenFOAMCase.setup_solver("simpleFoam")
```

```python
solver.set_boundary_conditions(boundary_conditions)

# Run the simulation
solver.run_simulation()

# Post-processing: visualizing the results
pressure_field = solver.get_field("pressure")
velocity_field = solver.get_field("velocity")

# Plotting pressure distribution
plt.figure(figsize=(8, 6))
plt.contourf(pressure_field, levels=20)
plt.colorbar(label="Pressure (Pa)")
plt.title("Pressure Distribution Over Aircraft Wing")
plt.show()
```

In this example:

- We use PyFoam to define the mesh, set boundary conditions, and run the solver.
- After the simulation, we use Matplotlib to visualize the pressure distribution over the aircraft wing.

This simple workflow demonstrates how Python can automate the setup, execution, and analysis of CFD simulations, making it an invaluable tool for engineers.

Challenges in CFD with Python

While Python offers powerful tools for CFD, there are some challenges:

- **Performance**: CFD simulations can be computationally intensive, especially for large domains with fine meshes. Using Python to solve CFD problems might require optimization techniques like parallel processing or using specialized high-performance computing clusters.

- **Complexity**: Setting up realistic CFD problems can be complex, requiring detailed knowledge of fluid mechanics and numerical methods.

- **Integration**: Although Python offers great flexibility, integrating it with established CFD software like OpenFOAM might require additional effort in terms of learning and configuring the software environment.

Python's ability to handle mathematical computations, automate workflows, and interact with powerful CFD tools like OpenFOAM makes it a valuable asset in the field of Computational Fluid Dynamics. Engineers can leverage Python to solve complex fluid flow problems, automate simulations, and visualize results with ease. By integrating Python with existing CFD solvers and libraries, engineers can achieve more efficient workflows, enhance productivity, and gain deeper insights into their designs.

In this chapter, we demonstrated how Python can be used for CFD applications in engineering, particularly in simulating airflow around an aircraft wing. As we continue to explore more advanced

CFD techniques and applications, Python remains a critical tool in shaping the future of fluid mechanics and aerodynamics in engineering.

Chapter 22: Image Processing in Engineering Applications

Image processing plays a crucial role in various engineering disciplines, from detecting defects in materials to analyzing medical images for health diagnostics. Engineers often work with images captured from sensors, microscopes, cameras, or scanners to extract valuable data that supports decision-making processes. Python, with its powerful libraries such as OpenCV, Pillow, and Scikit-Image, provides an accessible yet robust platform for implementing image processing tasks.

In this chapter, we will explore the basics of image processing in engineering applications, focusing on how Python can be used to analyze, enhance, and interpret images in practical engineering scenarios. Through real-world examples, we will showcase the application of image processing for defect detection and quality control in materials, a critical task in manufacturing, construction, and material science.

Image Processing Basics

Image processing involves manipulating and analyzing images to extract useful information or to improve the quality of the image. The process typically includes several stages, such as:

- **Image Acquisition:** Capturing images using sensors, cameras, or scanners.
- **Preprocessing:** Enhancing the image by removing noise, adjusting contrast, or converting it to grayscale.
- **Feature Extraction:** Identifying key patterns or structures in the image, such as edges, textures, or shapes.
- **Analysis and Interpretation:** Drawing s based on the processed image, such as identifying defects or measuring dimensions.

Python, as a flexible language with numerous libraries tailored for image processing, enables engineers to implement these stages effectively. Below are the key Python libraries used in image processing:

- **OpenCV (Open Source Computer Vision Library):** A powerful library that provides tools for real-time image processing, video analysis, feature detection, and machine learning. It is widely used for computer vision tasks, including object recognition, image segmentation, and motion tracking.
- **Pillow (PIL):** A user-friendly Python Imaging Library that simplifies image manipulation tasks such as opening, saving, and transforming images.
- **Scikit-Image:** Built on top of NumPy and SciPy, this library offers algorithms for image segmentation,

morphology, filtering, and more, which are essential for engineering applications.

Real-World Example: Analyzing Images from a Microscope or 3D Scanner to Detect Defects in Materials

In engineering, particularly in materials science and manufacturing, quality control is essential. Detecting surface defects or flaws in materials like metals, plastics, and composites can prevent costly failures in end-use products. With advances in imaging technologies such as microscopes and 3D scanners, engineers can now inspect the quality of materials at a microscopic level.

In this example, we will demonstrate how Python can be used to analyze images obtained from a microscope or a 3D scanner to detect material defects. The process involves the following steps:

1. **Image Acquisition:**
   - Capturing high-resolution images of the material surface using a microscope or a 3D scanner.

2. **Preprocessing the Image:**
   - **Grayscale Conversion:** For simplicity, we convert the color image to grayscale since defects are often more clearly visible in grayscale images.
   - **Noise Reduction:** Applying filters (e.g., Gaussian blur) to remove noise that might interfere with defect detection.

o **Thresholding:** Converting the grayscale image into a binary image where defects are highlighted (using methods like Otsu's thresholding).

3. **Edge Detection:**

   o Detecting the boundaries of defects in the material using edge-detection algorithms like the Canny Edge Detector. This step is crucial for identifying sharp boundaries between defective and non-defective areas of the material.

4. **Feature Extraction:**

   o Extracting features such as the size, shape, and location of the defects. Techniques such as contour detection help to outline the detected defects.

5. **Defect Detection and Analysis:**

   o Analyzing the extracted features to categorize defects (e.g., cracks, holes, or scratches).

   o Measuring the size or depth of defects and determining if they fall within acceptable limits.

6. **Visualization:**

   o Displaying the results with visual annotations, such as bounding boxes around defects, to help engineers quickly assess the material's quality.

Python Code Example for Defect Detection

python

```python
import cv2
import numpy as np

# Step 1: Load the image
image = cv2.imread('material_surface.jpg', cv2.IMREAD_GRAYSCALE)

# Step 2: Preprocessing - Noise reduction
blurred_image = cv2.GaussianBlur(image, (5, 5), 0)

# Step 3: Thresholding
_, threshold_image = cv2.threshold(blurred_image, 127, 255,
cv2.THRESH_BINARY)

# Step 4: Edge detection using Canny
edges = cv2.Canny(threshold_image, 100, 200)

# Step 5: Find contours (defects)
contours, _ = cv2.findContours(edges, cv2.RETR_EXTERNAL,
cv2.CHAIN_APPROX_SIMPLE)

# Step 6: Draw contours and measure defect size
output_image = cv2.cvtColor(image, cv2.COLOR_GRAY2BGR)
for contour in contours:
    area = cv2.contourArea(contour)
    if area > 500:  # Filter small contours
        cv2.drawContours(output_image, [contour], -1, (0, 255, 0), 2)
        # Optionally, measure the defect area
        print(f"Defect area: {area} pixels")

# Step 7: Show the results
```

```
cv2.imshow("Defect Detection", output_image)
cv2.waitKey(0)
cv2.destroyAllWindows()
```

Explanation of the Code:

1. **Load Image:** We load the image of the material surface using OpenCV's cv2.imread() function and convert it to grayscale.

2. **Noise Reduction:** We apply a Gaussian blur to smooth out the image and reduce noise.

3. **Thresholding:** We convert the image to a binary format where defects are highlighted.

4. **Edge Detection:** The Canny edge detection algorithm identifies sharp edges that correspond to defects.

5. **Contour Detection:** We find contours in the image that represent the boundaries of detected defects.

6. **Defect Area Measurement:** We calculate the area of each contour and filter out small ones that are unlikely to be defects.

7. **Visualization:** Finally, we draw the detected defects on the image and display the result using cv2.imshow().

Image processing in engineering applications using Python can provide powerful insights into the quality and integrity of materials, systems, and components. By leveraging Python libraries like

OpenCV and Scikit-Image, engineers can automate defect detection, conduct quality control more efficiently, and ensure that the manufactured products meet high standards. The ability to analyze and process images in real-time can also enhance other engineering processes, such as inspection, maintenance, and design optimization.

Chapter 23: Parallel Programming in Engineering

In engineering, many complex problems involve large-scale simulations, data analysis, and computational tasks that require significant processing power. These problems often take a long time to solve if only a single processor or core is used. Parallel programming enables the execution of multiple tasks or computations simultaneously, utilizing multiple processors or cores, thus significantly speeding up processes that would otherwise be time-prohibitive.

Python, through libraries like multiprocessing and threading, offers tools that allow engineers to develop parallelized solutions to computationally intensive problems. In this chapter, we will explore the fundamentals of parallel programming, how to implement parallelization in Python, and how it can be applied to solve real-world engineering challenges efficiently.

Introduction to Parallel Programming

Parallel programming involves dividing a task into smaller sub-tasks that can be executed simultaneously across multiple processors. It is a way to leverage multiple CPU cores to speed up computationally expensive tasks, making it particularly useful in fields like mechanical engineering, structural analysis, signal processing, and simulation modeling.

In Python, two main libraries—multiprocessing and threading—are used to implement parallel execution, each suited for different types of tasks.

- **Threading**: Threading allows you to run multiple threads in a single process. Threads are lighter than processes and are used when the tasks are I/O-bound, like reading data from files or making network requests. Threading can be useful for parallelizing tasks that do not require heavy CPU computation.

- **Multiprocessing**: Unlike threading, multiprocessing runs separate processes, each with its own memory space. This is ideal for CPU-bound tasks, such as heavy computations in simulations or data analysis. The multiprocessing module allows you to run multiple processes in parallel, fully utilizing multi-core processors.

Both libraries can be used to optimize engineering applications by parallelizing tasks that can be broken down into independent subtasks. Understanding how to use these tools effectively is critical for optimizing performance in real-world engineering problems.

Using Python's multiprocessing and threading Modules

- **Threading in Python**:

- o Threads are the smallest units of execution within a process.
- o In Python, the threading module allows for the creation and management of threads.
- o The Thread class is used to create a new thread and can execute a target function in parallel.
- o Threading is typically beneficial for tasks such as data I/O operations or applications where tasks are waiting for external resources (e.g., sensors, APIs).

Example of a basic threading program:

python

```python
import threading

def print_numbers():
    for i in range(1, 11):
        print(i)

def print_letters():
    for letter in 'abcdefghij':
        print(letter)

# Creating threads
thread1 = threading.Thread(target=print_numbers)
thread2 = threading.Thread(target=print_letters)

# Starting threads
```

```
thread1.start()
thread2.start()

# Waiting for both threads to finish
thread1.join()
thread2.join()
```

This example demonstrates how two threads can run concurrently to print numbers and letters simultaneously.

- **Multiprocessing in Python**:
  - In contrast to threading, the multiprocessing module creates separate processes with their own memory space.
  - This is beneficial for CPU-bound tasks that can run independently, such as simulations and mathematical computations.
  - The Pool class in multiprocessing allows you to distribute tasks across multiple processes, making it easier to parallelize large-scale operations.

Example of using multiprocessing:

python

```
from multiprocessing import Pool

def calculate_square(n):
    return n * n
```

```
if __name__ == "__main__":
    numbers = [1, 2, 3, 4, 5]
    with Pool(processes=3) as pool:
        results = pool.map(calculate_square, numbers)
    print(results)
```

In this example, the function calculate_square is applied to the list of numbers using multiple processes, allowing for parallel computation.

Real-World Example: Speeding Up Simulations or Calculations Using Parallel Processing

One area where parallel programming can be applied effectively in engineering is in the optimization and simulation of complex models. Let's consider a real-world example in mechanical engineering: **Finite Element Analysis (FEA)**.

Example: Parallelizing a Structural Simulation in FEA

Finite Element Analysis (FEA) is widely used in structural engineering to simulate the behavior of materials under different conditions, such as stress, strain, and deformation. FEA involves solving a large system of equations, which can take a significant amount of time when dealing with complex geometries and large datasets.

By applying parallel programming techniques, we can significantly reduce the time required to perform these simulations. The FEA process can be broken down into multiple smaller tasks, such as solving individual equations for different elements or subdomains of the model. Using Python's multiprocessing, each task can be assigned to a separate processor, allowing for parallel computation and faster simulation times.

Step-by-Step Parallelization of an FEA Simulation:

1. **Divide the Problem**: Break the entire FEA problem into smaller parts. For example, divide the mesh into several regions or break the matrix of equations into chunks.

2. **Parallel Task Assignment**: Use multiprocessing.Pool to distribute the work across multiple processes, with each process handling a portion of the matrix or solving a subset of the equations.

3. **Collect and Combine Results**: After the parallel processes finish, the results are combined and the final simulation output is produced.

Here's a simplified code snippet demonstrating how you might parallelize a basic FEA calculation:

python

```python
from multiprocessing import Pool

def solve_element(element_id):
    # Simulate solving an equation for a specific element
    result = element_id * 2  # Example computation
    return result
```

```python
def fea_simulation(element_count):
    with Pool(processes=4) as pool:
        results = pool.map(solve_element, range(element_count))
    return results


if __name__ == "__main__":
    # Assume we have 100 elements in our FEA model
    element_count = 100
    simulation_results = fea_simulation(element_count)
    print(simulation_results)
```

In this example, the solve_element function would represent the process of solving the equations for each element in the FEA model. By using the Pool.map method, we can distribute the task of solving equations across four processes, speeding up the entire simulation.

Parallel programming in Python is a powerful tool for engineers, allowing them to tackle computationally intensive problems efficiently. By using the multiprocessing and threading libraries, engineers can speed up simulations, data analysis, and large-scale calculations. This chapter highlighted the core concepts of parallel programming, provided an overview of how to implement it in Python, and demonstrated its application through a real-world example in finite element analysis. With these skills, engineers can significantly improve the performance and scalability of their computational models and simulations.

Chapter 24: Python in Engineering Design and CAD Systems

In the world of engineering, Computer-Aided Design (CAD) systems play a crucial role in the development of products, structures, and systems across various fields. These tools allow engineers to create detailed, accurate digital models of physical objects, systems, and components. However, while CAD software provides powerful capabilities for visualization and design, there are many tasks that can benefit from automation and customization, which is where Python comes into play.

Python has emerged as a versatile tool that can be used to automate repetitive tasks in CAD systems, enhance design calculations, and integrate external data and algorithms. Through scripting, engineers can control CAD software, perform complex calculations, optimize designs, and even generate customized reports. This chapter explores how Python can be integrated with engineering design tools, particularly CAD systems, to streamline workflows and improve design efficiency.

Using Python in Engineering Design Tools

Python is an accessible and powerful language for automating design processes in many popular CAD software platforms, including AutoCAD, SolidWorks, Rhino, and others. These CAD tools often provide APIs or scripting interfaces that allow engineers to interact with the software programmatically. By learning to use Python for scripting in these environments, engineers can:

1. **Automate Design Tasks:** Python can be used to automate repetitive design steps, such as creating standard components, modifying designs based on parameters, or generating design variations for optimization studies.

2. **Integrate Design Calculations:** Python can be used to perform complex engineering calculations (e.g., stress analysis, thermal simulations, and material selection) directly within the CAD environment. This makes it easier to check design feasibility and ensure that calculations are always up to date.

3. **Enhance Customization and Flexibility:** Python allows engineers to customize the behavior of the CAD tool, enabling tailored solutions that meet the specific needs of a project. Whether you need to create parametric models or develop custom design tools, Python provides the flexibility to enhance the standard CAD interface.

4. **Develop Design Optimization Algorithms:** Python is also used to develop and implement optimization algorithms for

design problems. Engineers can use Python to refine designs based on various performance criteria (e.g., weight reduction, strength enhancement, material cost), which is essential for efficient and sustainable engineering design.

Real-World Example: Automating Design Calculations for Mechanical Parts in CAD Software Using Python

Let's consider a practical example in which Python is used to automate design calculations for a mechanical part within a CAD environment, such as SolidWorks or AutoCAD.

Problem:

In the design of a mechanical component, engineers frequently need to perform various calculations for material selection, stress analysis, and load-bearing capabilities. These calculations are essential for determining whether a design is structurally sound and can withstand the required conditions. However, performing these calculations manually for each design iteration is time-consuming and error-prone.

Solution:

By integrating Python with the CAD software, engineers can automate the calculation process and ensure that all necessary computations are performed automatically whenever the design changes. For example, Python can be used to:

1. **Automate Material Property Input:** Engineers can write a Python script to input material properties (such as Young's modulus, yield strength, and density) into the CAD software for use in subsequent calculations. The script can also retrieve material data from an external database or file.

2. **Perform Stress and Strain Calculations:** Python can be used to calculate stress, strain, and other mechanical properties based on the geometry of the part, such as dimensions, shape, and applied loads. These calculations can be run automatically after every design change, ensuring real-time feedback.

3. **Integrate Finite Element Analysis (FEA):** Python can be used to integrate with FEA software or libraries like PyNastran, which allows engineers to perform more detailed simulations of how the part will perform under various conditions. This can include stress testing, thermal analysis, and fatigue simulations.

4. **Generate Design Reports:** Python can automate the generation of reports that summarize the results of the calculations, such as stress values, material performance, and safety factors. These reports can be generated in PDF or Excel format, allowing engineers to quickly share results with colleagues or clients.

Implementation in Python:

python

```python
import math
import numpy as np

# Define material properties
yield_strength = 250  # in MPa
elastic_modulus = 210000  # in MPa (Pa for material)

# Define part dimensions
diameter = 50  # in mm
length = 200  # in mm
applied_force = 1000  # in N

# Calculate cross-sectional area of the part (circular cross-section)
area = math.pi * (diameter / 2) ** 2  # in mm^2

# Convert to meters for standard units
area = area * 1e-6  # mm^2 to m^2

# Calculate stress (σ = Force / Area)
stress = applied_force / area  # in N/m^2 or Pascals (Pa)

# Perform basic validation
if stress > yield_strength * 1e6:  # Convert MPa to Pa
    print("Warning: The part exceeds yield strength!")
else:
    print(f"The stress on the part is {stress / 1e6} MPa, within safe limits.")
```

```
# Calculate deflection using basic formula for a cantilever beam (δ = FL^3 /
3EI)
deflection = (applied_force * length**3) / (3 * elastic_modulus * area)
print(f"The deflection of the part is {deflection} meters.")
```

Explanation:

- In the code above, Python is used to automate the calculation of stress and deflection for a mechanical part, such as a beam under an applied force.
- The script defines material properties (e.g., yield strength and elastic modulus) and part dimensions (e.g., diameter and length).
- The calculations are performed based on basic mechanical engineering principles, and results are printed to ensure that the part meets the required specifications.
- The Python script can be integrated with a CAD software like SolidWorks using an API to retrieve geometry and update the model automatically based on the calculated values.

:

By leveraging Python in the design phase, engineers can enhance the productivity of their workflows, reduce human error, and ensure that design calculations are always up to date. The ability to automate repetitive tasks, perform real-time simulations, and generate optimized designs based on data-driven feedback can significantly improve the efficiency of engineering projects. Python's versatility and accessibility make it an invaluable tool in the field of engineering design, allowing engineers to solve complex problems with ease.

Chapter 25: Future Trends – Python in Emerging Engineering Fields

Python has established itself as a powerful and versatile language in various engineering disciplines, from mechanical and civil engineering to electrical and aerospace engineering. However, as technological advancements continue to reshape industries, Python is also evolving to meet the demands of new and emerging fields. In particular, the convergence of Artificial Intelligence (AI), the Internet of Things (IoT), and Industry 4.0 represents a significant shift in engineering practices, where automation, connectivity, and data-driven decision-making are taking center stage.

This chapter will explore the future of Python in engineering, focusing on how it is adapting to emerging trends like AI, IoT, and Industry 4.0. We will also delve into a real-world example of building an IoT application to monitor and control machinery using Python, demonstrating how engineers can leverage the language for next-generation technologies.

Future of Python in Engineering

As industries increasingly rely on advanced technologies such as AI, IoT, and automation, Python's role in engineering continues to expand. Below, we explore some of the key ways Python is evolving and shaping the future of engineering.

1. Python in Artificial Intelligence (AI)

AI is transforming engineering by enabling machines and systems to learn from data, make decisions autonomously, and improve over time. Python has become the go-to language for developing AI applications due to its rich ecosystem of libraries and frameworks.

- **Machine Learning and Deep Learning**: Python libraries like Scikit-learn, TensorFlow, Keras, and PyTorch are at the forefront of machine learning (ML) and deep learning (DL). Engineers can use these libraries to build predictive models, automate decision-making, and enhance design processes with AI-driven insights.
- **Optimization and Control**: In engineering applications such as robotics, autonomous vehicles, and manufacturing, AI is used to optimize systems, improve efficiency, and reduce waste. Python's capabilities in AI and optimization are allowing engineers to solve more complex problems and automate tasks that were previously labor-intensive.

As Python continues to evolve, its integration with AI tools will make it even more essential for solving engineering problems in the fields of automation, predictive maintenance, and smart systems.

2. Python in Internet of Things (IoT)

The Internet of Things (IoT) involves the interconnection of physical devices (such as machinery, sensors, and appliances) through the internet. In engineering, IoT has revolutionized how systems are monitored, controlled, and optimized in real-time.

- **IoT Sensors and Data Collection**: Python is frequently used to interface with IoT devices, gather sensor data, and send it to cloud-based platforms for processing. With libraries such as paho-mqtt and requests, Python makes it easy to communicate with IoT sensors and collect large volumes of real-time data.

- **Automation and Control**: Python is also employed to process data from IoT devices and use it for real-time decision-making and system control. For instance, an engineer can use Python to program an IoT-enabled system that autonomously adjusts machine parameters based on sensor readings.

In the future, Python's ability to integrate with IoT systems will continue to play a crucial role in building smarter, more efficient engineering systems, where real-time data and automation are at the heart of operations.

3. Python in Industry 4.0

Industry 4.0 refers to the ongoing revolution in manufacturing and industrial practices, where digital technologies such as AI, IoT, automation, and data analytics are transforming production systems. Python is a key enabler of Industry 4.0, providing engineers with the tools to build smart factories and interconnected systems.

- **Smart Manufacturing**: Python supports the development of smart manufacturing systems that rely on sensors, robotics, and data analysis. It can be used to automate factory workflows, optimize production schedules, and predict machine failures before they occur.

- **Data Analytics for Decision-Making**: In Industry 4.0, vast amounts of data are generated from sensors and machines. Python's data analysis capabilities, particularly with libraries like Pandas, NumPy, and SciPy, allow engineers to derive insights from this data to make informed decisions that improve efficiency and reduce costs.

Python's role in Industry 4.0 will continue to grow as more companies adopt connected, automated systems, and engineers leverage Python to design and optimize these systems.

Real-World Example: Building an IoT Application to Monitor and Control Machinery via Python

One of the most exciting applications of Python in engineering is in the development of IoT-based systems that allow engineers to monitor and control machinery remotely. In this real-world example, we will demonstrate how Python can be used to build a simple IoT application to monitor the temperature and vibration levels of a machine and control its operation.

Problem:

Imagine an industrial machine that operates in a factory. The machine's performance needs to be monitored for temperature and vibration to ensure it is operating safely. If the temperature exceeds a certain threshold, or if vibrations are detected beyond acceptable levels, the machine needs to be shut down automatically to prevent damage.

Solution:

We can use Python to interface with IoT sensors (e.g., temperature and vibration sensors), collect real-time data, and control the machine's operation based on predefined thresholds. This system will use MQTT (Message Queuing Telemetry Transport) for communication between the sensors and the control system.

Step 1: Install Dependencies

First, install the necessary libraries for Python to communicate with the IoT sensors and the control system:

bash

```
pip install paho-mqtt
```

Step 2: Set Up MQTT Broker

For simplicity, we'll use a local MQTT broker (e.g., Mosquitto) to manage communication between the sensors and the control system. You can install Mosquitto on your local machine or use a cloud-based broker.

Step 3: Monitor Sensors and Control Machinery

The following Python code demonstrates how to monitor the temperature and vibration of the machine and send control signals based on the sensor readings:

```python
python

import paho.mqtt.client as mqtt
import random
import time

# Define thresholds
TEMP_THRESHOLD = 75  # in degrees Celsius
VIBRATION_THRESHOLD = 10  # vibration level (arbitrary unit)

# MQTT settings
BROKER = "localhost"
PORT = 1883
TOPIC_TEMP = "machine/temperature"
TOPIC_VIBRATION = "machine/vibration"
TOPIC_CONTROL = "machine/control"

# Function to simulate reading sensor data
```

```python
def read_temperature():
    return random.uniform(60, 90)  # Simulate a temperature range

def read_vibration():
    return random.uniform(0, 15)  # Simulate a vibration range


# Function to handle incoming messages
def on_message(client, userdata, message):
    print(f"Received message on {message.topic}: {message.payload.decode()}")
    if message.topic == TOPIC_CONTROL:
        if message.payload.decode() == "shutdown":
            print("Shutting down the machine...")
            # Code to shut down the machine
            exit(0)


# Set up MQTT client
client = mqtt.Client()
client.on_message = on_message


# Connect to broker
client.connect(BROKER, PORT, 60)
client.subscribe(TOPIC_CONTROL)


# Main loop to monitor machine
try:
    while True:
        # Read sensor data
        temperature = read_temperature()
        vibration = read_vibration()
```

```
# Publish sensor data to MQTT broker
client.publish(TOPIC_TEMP, temperature)
client.publish(TOPIC_VIBRATION, vibration)

# Check if any of the thresholds are exceeded
if temperature > TEMP_THRESHOLD:
    print(f"Warning: Temperature {temperature}°C exceeds threshold! Shutting down machine.")
    client.publish(TOPIC_CONTROL, "shutdown")

if vibration > VIBRATION_THRESHOLD:
    print(f"Warning: Vibration {vibration} exceeds threshold! Shutting down machine.")
    client.publish(TOPIC_CONTROL, "shutdown")

# Process incoming messages
client.loop()

time.sleep(2)  # Simulate a delay before reading the sensors again
except KeyboardInterrupt:
    print("Program interrupted")
```

Explanation:

- **MQTT Communication**: We use the paho-mqtt library to set up an MQTT client, subscribe to sensor topics, and control the machine by publishing messages to the control topic.

- **Sensor Simulation**: We simulate sensor data for temperature and vibration using random number generation.

197

In a real-world application, these values would come from actual IoT sensors.

- **Threshold Checking**: The script continuously checks if the temperature or vibration exceeds predefined thresholds. If so, it publishes a "shutdown" message to the MQTT broker, which triggers the control system to shut down the machine.

Step 4:

In this example, Python facilitates the development of an IoT application that monitors and controls machinery in real time. By leveraging MQTT for communication and Python for automation, engineers can create efficient systems for managing complex operations, such as monitoring machinery and responding to sensor data in real-time.

This example highlights Python's growing role in the IoT and Industry 4.0 revolution, where it can be used to create interconnected, intelligent systems that enhance operational efficiency, improve safety, and reduce downtime in industrial settings.

Python is at the forefront of many emerging engineering fields, including AI, IoT, and Industry 4.0. As the demand for smart, connected systems grows, Python's versatility and extensive ecosystem of libraries will continue to enable engineers to tackle new challenges, optimize operations, and drive innovations.

Through real-world examples like the IoT-based machinery monitoring application, this chapter has demonstrated how Python is shaping the future of engineering, making it more automated, data-driven, and efficient.

Chapter 26: Python for Automation and Smart Manufacturing

Introduction to Automation and Smart Manufacturing

- **What is Smart Manufacturing?**
  - Smart manufacturing represents a transformative shift in industrial operations, integrating advanced technologies like sensors, robotics, AI, and real-time data analysis to create efficient, self-regulating production systems. It is part of the broader Industry 4.0 movement, which focuses on digital transformation in manufacturing.
  - The core features of smart manufacturing include: increased operational efficiency, real-time monitoring, predictive maintenance, enhanced quality control, and optimization of production processes. These systems are powered by real-time data collection from machines, sensors, and connected devices.

- **The Role of Automation in Modern Engineering**
  - Automation is the backbone of smart manufacturing. It involves using control systems (like PLCs and SCADA systems) to perform tasks traditionally

carried out by human operators. With automation, industries can increase speed, consistency, precision, and safety while reducing human errors and operational costs.

- o Modern manufacturing involves multiple levels of automation:

    - **Basic Automation:** Automating repetitive tasks like assembly line operations.

    - **Advanced Automation:** Involving more complex systems like robotics, autonomous vehicles, and self-optimizing production lines.

- o Automation also includes real-time data feedback loops that allow machines to adjust based on ongoing conditions.

- **How Python Fits into Automation Workflows and the Industrial Internet of Things (IIoT)**

    - o Python has become a go-to language in the automation space due to its simplicity, readability, and vast ecosystem of libraries and frameworks. Python is well-suited for controlling machines, processing sensor data, and interacting with automation hardware in industrial settings.

    - o The **Industrial Internet of Things (IIoT)** refers to the integration of smart devices and sensors into industrial systems. Python can bridge the gap between various IIoT devices by enabling data collection, processing, and decision-making.

- o Key features of Python in IIoT:
  - **Interfacing with Sensors:** Python can easily interface with various sensors (temperature, pressure, vibration, etc.) to collect data from the production floor.
  - **Data Analysis and Processing:** Python can analyze data in real time using libraries like Pandas, NumPy, and SciPy to extract meaningful insights and automate decision-making.
  - **Communication Protocols:** Python supports various communication protocols like MQTT, Modbus, and OPC-UA to facilitate communication between machines and control systems in IIoT environments.

Using Python for Factory Automation

- **Controlling Machines and Robots Using Python**
  - o Python can be used to control robotic arms, conveyor belts, and other machinery in

manufacturing environments. Libraries like PySerial, pyModbus, and OPC-UA allow Python to communicate with PLCs, robotic controllers, and industrial machines over serial or Ethernet connections.

- o **Example Use Case:** Automating the movement of robotic arms in a packaging plant. Python scripts can send commands to move the robot along a predefined path, pick up items, and place them in boxes based on sensor data.

- o **Automation Protocols and Libraries:** Python interacts with machine controllers through industrial communication protocols. Libraries like **PyModbus** for Modbus RTU/TCP and **python-opcua** for OPC-UA can be leveraged to send and receive commands, control actuators, and monitor sensor data.

- **Integration with Programmable Logic Controllers (PLCs)**

  - o PLCs are widely used in manufacturing plants for automation and controlling machinery. Python can interface with PLCs via communication protocols like **Modbus, OPC-UA,** or **Ethernet/IP** to trigger specific actions or retrieve data.

  - o **PLC Programming and Python Integration:**

- Traditional PLC programming involves ladder logic or structured text. However, integrating Python allows engineers to extend the PLC's functionality by introducing higher-level logic and advanced data processing capabilities.

- Python scripts can be used to receive data from PLCs, process it, and make decisions, such as adjusting machine parameters or shutting down equipment if safety thresholds are exceeded.

- Real-time data can be monitored through Python scripts, and the system can adjust parameters automatically, creating a dynamic feedback loop.

- **SCADA Systems for Automated Processes**
  - **Supervisory Control and Data Acquisition (SCADA)** systems are used for monitoring and controlling industrial processes. SCADA systems gather data from PLCs, sensors, and other devices, and Python can be used to interface with SCADA systems to enhance data processing, visualization, and automation.

- Python libraries like pyModbus and pysnmp can be used to interface with SCADA systems, enabling real-time data collection and decision-making.

- **Example Application:** Python can be used to monitor the performance of machines in real time and automatically adjust machine settings based on sensor data. If a particular machine's performance drops below a set threshold (e.g., temperature, speed, or pressure), Python can trigger corrective actions such as increasing cooling or slowing down production speed.

Real-World Example: Building a Python Application to Monitor Production Lines, Detect Anomalies, and Adjust Machinery Settings

- **Objective:**
  - The goal of this real-world example is to demonstrate how Python can be used in a production line environment to monitor machine performance, detect anomalies, and automatically adjust machinery settings to maintain optimal performance.
- **Components Involved:**

- o **Sensors:** Temperature, vibration, and pressure sensors on critical machines in the production line.

- o **PLC Communication:** Interfacing with a PLC to retrieve machine data and send commands.

- o **Python Libraries:**

  - PyModbus: For Modbus communication between Python and the PLC.

  - NumPy: For data processing and anomaly detection algorithms.

  - Matplotlib: For real-time visualization of sensor data.

  - Scikit-learn: For implementing a machine learning-based anomaly detection algorithm.

- **Step-by-Step Workflow:**

1. **Data Collection:**

   - Python communicates with the PLC over Modbus or OPC-UA to collect real-time data from sensors. The data may include temperature, vibration, pressure, and machine speed.

   - This data is collected at regular intervals and stored in a Pandas DataFrame for processing.

2. **Data Preprocessing:**

   - The collected sensor data is cleaned, and any missing values are handled. If sensor data is noisy, Python's SciPy can be used to apply filters or smoothing techniques to clean up the data.

3.   **Anomaly Detection:**

- A machine learning model is trained using historical data to detect abnormal behavior. For example, if a machine's vibration exceeds a certain threshold, it could indicate a malfunction.

- Python's Scikit-learn can be used to apply anomaly detection algorithms such as Isolation Forest or One-Class SVM to flag irregularities in the sensor data.

4.   **Automatic Adjustment:**

- When an anomaly is detected, Python can trigger a response by sending control signals to the PLC to adjust machine settings, such as lowering the speed, increasing the cooling rate, or stopping a faulty machine.

5.   **Real-Time Visualization:**

- Python's Matplotlib can visualize the sensor data in real-time, allowing operators to monitor the system's health visually.

- A dashboard can be built using Python's Dash library to provide a comprehensive view of the production line status, including warnings and error reports.

6. **Reporting and Logging:**

- After every automated adjustment, Python logs the actions taken and generates a report for future analysis. These logs can be saved in CSV or database formats and analyzed periodically for improvements.

- **Impact:**

  o This Python application helps ensure continuous operation of the production line by detecting problems early and minimizing downtime. With real-time monitoring and automatic adjustments, the system increases efficiency and lowers the risk of unexpected failures.

This chapter emphasizes Python's critical role in enhancing automation and improving operational efficiency in manufacturing processes, demonstrating how engineers can leverage Python for both immediate troubleshooting and long-term optimization in industrial environments.

Chapter 27: Python for Engineering Data Security and Privacy

Importance of Data Security in Engineering

- **The Growing Need for Data Security in Engineering**
  - As the engineering sector embraces digital transformation, the amount of sensitive data generated and shared across platforms continues to grow. From design specifications and research data to control systems and sensor logs, protecting intellectual property, personal data, and proprietary information is critical.
  - Engineering data is increasingly stored and processed digitally through cloud services, local databases, or connected devices in fields such as mechanical, civil, and electrical engineering. With the rise of automation, smart manufacturing, and IoT (Internet of Things), securing data from cyber threats has become paramount.
  - Security challenges for engineers include protecting sensitive data against unauthorized access, maintaining data integrity, ensuring secure

communication across networks, and preventing data breaches that could impact operations or safety.

- **The Role of Python in Engineering Data Security**
  - ○ Python has emerged as one of the most widely used programming languages for developing secure applications due to its simplicity, flexibility, and the extensive libraries it offers. Python's broad ecosystem includes powerful libraries and frameworks that can be leveraged to implement security features like encryption, authentication, and secure data transfer.
  - ○ Python's rich support for cryptography, secure socket programming, and data validation makes it a preferred choice for engineers looking to integrate data security measures into their systems. Whether it's ensuring secure communication in industrial IoT systems, encrypting design data, or safeguarding sensitive research results, Python has tools and libraries suited for all engineering needs.

Cryptography and Secure Communication in Python

- **Introduction to Cryptography in Engineering**

- Cryptography is the practice of securing data through techniques such as encryption and decryption. In engineering, cryptography is essential to protect sensitive information, especially in industries like aerospace, automotive, and manufacturing, where unauthorized access to design data or control systems could lead to significant risks.

- Common cryptographic techniques used in engineering applications include:
    - **Symmetric encryption**: Using the same key for both encryption and decryption, suitable for high-performance applications.
    - **Asymmetric encryption**: Using a public/private key pair, often used for secure communication over open networks.
    - **Hashing**: Generating a fixed-length value (hash) from data, useful for verifying data integrity.

- **Using Python Libraries for Cryptography**
    - Python offers a variety of libraries to handle cryptographic operations:
        - **PyCryptodome**: A low-level cryptographic library that provides various encryption algorithms (AES, DES, RSA), hashing

algorithms (SHA, MD5), and functionalities for secure key management and message signing.

- **Fernet (from the cryptography library)**: A higher-level encryption system providing symmetric encryption with authenticated encryption.

- **SSL/TLS**: Python's ssl module allows for secure communication over networks, commonly used for securing HTTP traffic (HTTPS).

o **Example Code Snippet: Encrypting and Decrypting Data using PyCryptodome**

python

```
from Crypto.Cipher import AES
from Crypto.Util.Padding import pad, unpad
from Crypto.Random import get_random_bytes

# Key generation and cipher setup
key = get_random_bytes(16)  # AES-128 bit key
cipher = AES.new(key, AES.MODE_CBC)

# Data to encrypt
data = b"Sensitive engineering design data"
ciphertext = cipher.encrypt(pad(data, AES.block_size))
```

```
# Decryption process
decipher = AES.new(key, AES.MODE_CBC, iv=cipher.iv)
decrypted_data      =      unpad(decipher.decrypt(ciphertext),
AES.block_size)

print("Original:", data)
print("Decrypted:", decrypted_data)
```

- In this example, the PyCryptodome library encrypts and decrypts design data securely, demonstrating the importance of encryption in protecting confidential information in engineering.

- **Secure Communication Protocols in Python**
  - **Implementing Secure Socket Communication**: Using Python's ssl module, engineers can establish secure, encrypted communication between devices and servers. This is especially useful in Industrial IoT (IIoT) applications where remote devices must exchange critical control data securely.
    - Example of Secure HTTP Request Using Python:

```python
import ssl
import urllib.request
```

```
context = ssl.create_default_context()
url = "https://example.com/data"

# Send a secure request to the server
response            =           urllib.request.urlopen(url,
context=context)
data = response.read()
print(data)
```

- **Authentication and Access Control**
  - Python can also be used to implement secure user authentication systems, allowing engineers to protect their systems from unauthorized access. This can be done using libraries like **Flask-Login** for web-based applications or **OAuth2** for API access control.
  - **Example**: Using the hashlib library to securely store user credentials and verify login attempts using hashing:

python

```
import hashlib

def hash_password(password):
    return hashlib.sha256(password.encode()).hexdigest()

# Storing the hashed password
stored_password = hash_password("securepassword")
```

```
# Verifying the entered password
entered_password = "securepassword"
if hash_password(entered_password) == stored_password:
    print("Access Granted")
else:
    print("Access Denied")
```

Real-World Example: Building a Python Application to Encrypt and Securely Transmit Data

- **Problem Overview**
  - Engineers working with design data, sensor logs, and control system configurations need to ensure their data is encrypted before transmission to protect against cyber threats like man-in-the-middle attacks.
  - This example demonstrates how Python can be used to securely encrypt design files, and transmit them over a network, ensuring the confidentiality and integrity of the data.
- **Step-by-Step Breakdown**

1. **Data Encryption**:
   - Use **PyCryptodome** to encrypt sensitive files (e.g., CAD files, design specifications).

- Generate a key and use it to encrypt the file before transmission.

2. **Secure Transmission**:
   - Use Python's **ssl** and **socket** libraries to establish a secure communication channel with the recipient system.

3. **Decryption on the Receiver Side**:
   - Once the encrypted data is received, use the same encryption key to decrypt and read the design files securely.

- **Code Implementation**:

python

```python
import socket
import ssl
from Crypto.Cipher import AES
from Crypto.Random import get_random_bytes

# Step 1: Encrypt data using AES
def encrypt_data(data):
    key = get_random_bytes(16)
    cipher = AES.new(key, AES.MODE_CBC)
    ciphertext = cipher.encrypt(pad(data.encode(), AES.block_size))
    return cipher.iv + ciphertext  # Send IV with the encrypted data

# Step 2: Establish a secure connection
context = ssl.create_default_context(ssl.Purpose.CLIENT_AUTH)
```

```
with socket.create_connection(('receiver.com', 443)) as sock:
    with context.wrap_socket(sock, server_hostname='receiver.com') as secure_sock:
        encrypted_data = encrypt_data("Confidential engineering design data")
        secure_sock.sendall(encrypted_data)
        print("Data sent securely!")


# On the receiving side, use the same key and IV to decrypt the data.
```

- **Benefits of Using Python for Data Security in Engineering**

  o Python's simplicity, flexibility, and wide range of libraries make it a powerful tool for implementing robust security protocols in engineering applications.

  o From encryption and secure communication to user authentication, Python helps engineers ensure that their sensitive data remains safe from unauthorized access during transmission and storage.

By leveraging Python's powerful security capabilities, engineers can build resilient, secure systems that protect critical data and maintain confidentiality, ensuring compliance with industry standards and safeguarding intellectual property in an increasingly connected world.